The Golf Book

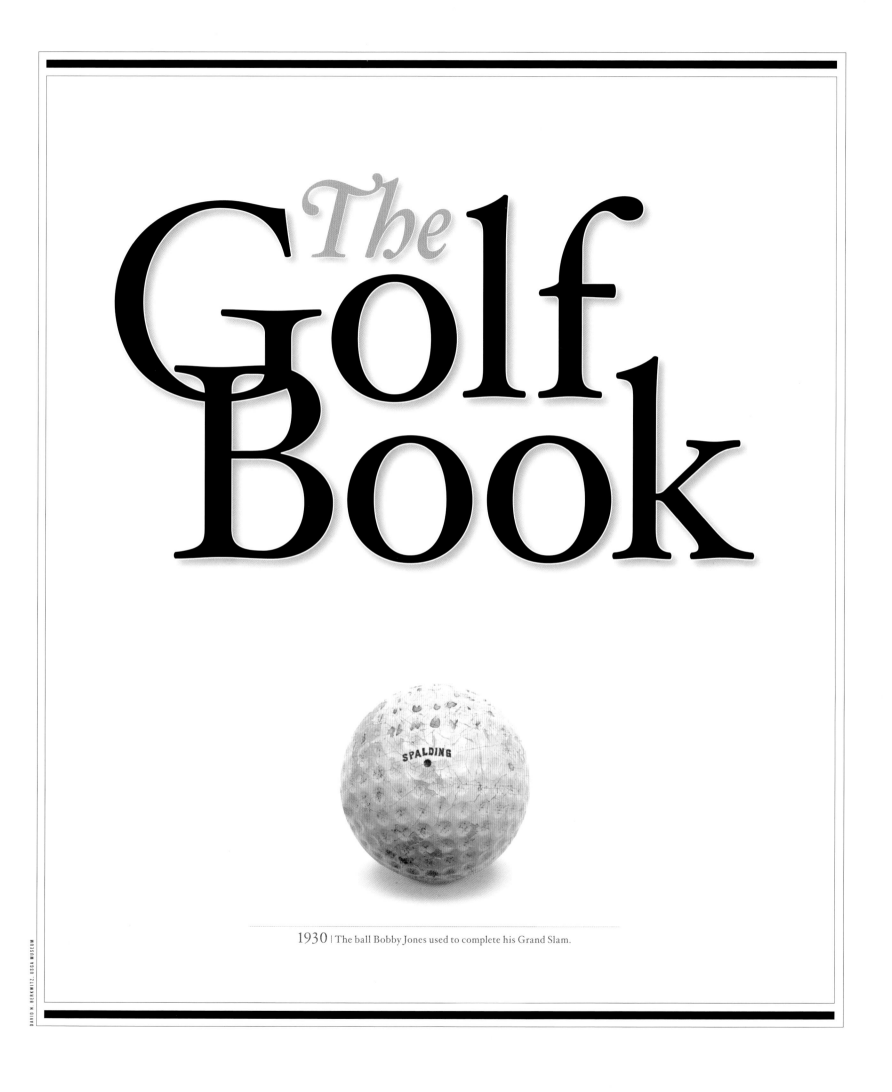

1930 | The ball Bobby Jones used to complete his Grand Slam.

BOBBY JONES
British Amateur champion
1930
Courtesy of EMORY UNIVERSITY

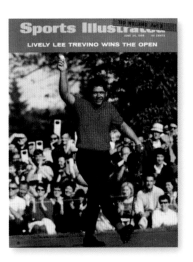

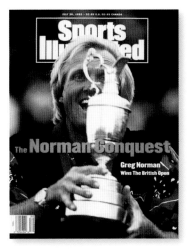

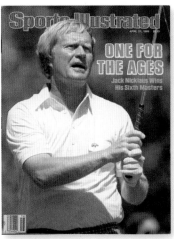

The Golf Book

KEVIN COOK
Editor

STEVEN HOFFMAN
Designer

JIM GORANT *Senior Editor*   DAVID SABINO *Associate Editor*

CRISTINA SCALET *Photo Editor*   JENNIFER GRAD *Assistant Photo Editor*

KEVIN KERR *Copy Editor*   JOSH DENKIN *Associate Designer*

SARAH KWAK *Reporter*   STEFANIE KAUFMAN *Project Manager*

USGA MUSEUM, WORLD GOLF HALL OF FAME
Archives and Historical Reference

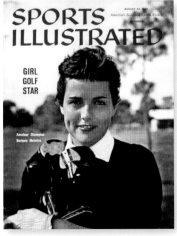

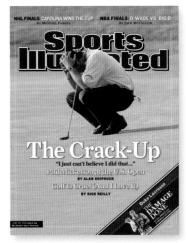

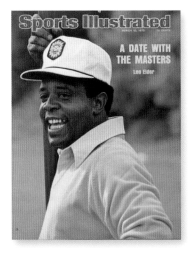

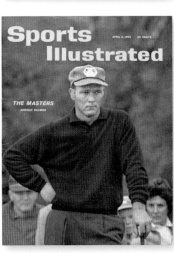

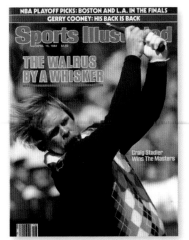

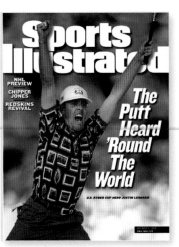

Sports Illustrated Contents

JACK NICKLAUS
Posing as a shady character
1967
Photograph by WALTER IOOSS JR.

RAKE IRON
For shots from rough or water
1905
Photograph by DAVID N. BERKWITZ

MAS

Articles & Laws in playing the Golf

1. You must Tee your Ball within a Club length of the Hole

2. Your Tee must be upon the Ground

3. You are not to change the Ball Which you Strike off the Tee.

4. You are not to remove Stones, Bones or any Break Club for the Sake of playing your Ball, Except upon the fair Green, and that only within a Club length of your Ball.

5. If your Ball come among Water, Or any Watery filth, You are at Liberty, to take out your Ball, and throwing it behind the Hazard ~~six yards at least~~ three yards at least, You may play it with any Club, and allow your Adversary a Stroke, for so getting out your Ball.

6. If your Balls be found any Where touching one another, You are to lift the first Ball, till You play the last.

7. At Holeing, You are to play Your Ball honestly for the Hole, And not to play upon your Adversary's Ball, not lying in your Way to the Hole

8. If You should lose your Ball, by its being taken Up, or any Other way You are to go back to the Spot, Where you Struck last, and drop another Ball, and Allow your Adversary a Stroke for the Misfortune

9. No Man at Holeing his Ball, is to be Allowed to Mark his Way to the Hole with his Club or any thing else.

10. If a Ball be Stop'd by any person, Horse, Dog, or any thing else, the Ball so Stop'd Must be played Where it lyes.

11. If You draw your Club, in Order to Strike, and proceed so far in thee Stroke as to be bringing down your Club; if then your Club shall break, in any Way, it is to be Accounted a Stroke.

12. He, Whose Ball lyes furthest from the Hole is Obliged to play first

13. Neither Trench, Ditch, or Dyke made for the preservation of the Links, Nor the Scholars holes or the Soldiers Lines, Shall be Accounted a Hazard, But the Ball is to be taken out, Teed and played with any Iron Club.

FOREWORD

BY ROY BLOUNT JR.

WE'RE TALKING GOLF

*No other sport generates language the way
golf does—much of it printable, all hinting at the
hickory-hearted essence of a strange old game*

THE BRASSIE. THE MASHIE. THE SPOON. THE NIBLICK. THE CLEEK. They're gone! And it's a rotten shame. You can hear all those old clubs rattling about in the golf bag of history. According to *The Historical Dictionary of Golfing Terms*, by Peter Davies, *cleek* is an old Scots word for "crook, walking stick with a hook." The light narrow-bladed iron in question "was sometimes also spelled *click*, and so associated with the sound of the impact of club on ball." *Nib* is an old Scots word for "beak," and *niblick*—referring to the original stubby-headed wooden version of this club—probably meant

THE SOCIETY of St. Andrews Golfers used 343 words to lay out the game's rules (left) in 1754, when bones, dogs and "watery filth" were common hazards.

"short-nose." With a niblick you could root a ball out of a bad lie like a pig snouting up truffles (and put a solid lick on it).

Those clubs' modern equivalents are just woods (made of steel or titanium) and irons, with numbers. Where's the romance there? Where's the onomatopoeia?

Or maybe I'm reaching, I'm pressing. I'm trying to revel in golf language, and all I am doing is foozling.

To *foozle*, of course, is to bungle a shot. *The Historical Dictionary of Golfing Terms* leaves the etymology of *foozle* at "origin unknown," but Webster's Third unabridged raises the possibility that *foozle* may come from the German dialect verb *fuseln*, "to work hurriedly or poorly."

So. Let me do a little waggle here. (*Waggle*, referring to a preliminary flourishing of the club before grounding it, goes back at least as far as 1890. Before that, did people not waggle? Did they call waggling something else? We don't know.)

Loosen up my wrists. Get a good balance. Relaxed, natural.

I might mention that neither of the two groundbreaking golf stories that I wrote for SPORTS ILLUSTRATED....

O.K., not groundbreaking. How about divot-taking? *Divot* is just an old Scottish term for a chunk of turf. Roofs used to be made of them. *Taking* a divot however does not imply that you can carry it home with you, to start a new lawn with. Or a roof garden.

Maybe my stories weren't divot-taking, even. But surely not just sclaffing. To *sclaff* is to unintentionally hit the ground before the ball. The very sound of it jangles my wrists. Not to mention hips and....

Nor were those stories chili-dipping. A *chili-dip* is a mishit somehow evocative of the fact that when you try to dip up a lot of chili with a taco chip, you don't get a lot of chili. On your taco chip. Should've gone with the five-iron, I suppose.

Start over. Shift weight back and forth. But no *happy feet*. Let the club swing itself. Yeah, right.

They were stories that I wrote for SI some years ago. Neither of them, I might mention, has been deemed worthy of inclusion in this book.

And I believe I know why: because I don't know anything about golf. Oh, I have tried to play it. One of those two stories was about taking part in the late Chet Atkins's celebrity golf tournament, more specifically about how hard it is to convince the others in your foursome of strangers that you

can't play golf. Until you hit your first shot. My other SI golf story was investigative—I asked ordinary citizens of Augusta what effect the Masters tournament had on them. On Saturday night of Masters week, outside the Sans Souci apartment complex, where a party was going on, a pretty young woman sat in a Volkswagen, crying.

Her husband wouldn't let her go out by herself, she said, and he worked at night and she worked during the day, and she wasn't happy being married, and she'd been drinking, and her husband had a gun, and she liked to dance, and she had to go home.

"What," she was asked as gently as possible, "does the Masters mean to you?"

She spoke in terms of traffic. "The Masters," she pondered before starting up her car to go home. She was still crying. "The Masters means 45 minutes to make an eight-minute drive."

So often golf is attended by sadness. That is as broadly as I intend to generalize. I won't try to tell you that just as baseball is a four-pointed pastoral journey from home back on around to home again, golf is a reenactment of the eternal quest for beachfront property. What with the sand and all.

No. My game is not big philosophical ideas. It is words.

Take *golf*. You may have assumed that the word was *flog* backwards, as in self-flagellation. Or a compression of "Gosh all Friday" or some stronger oath. But no, the Scots probably borrowed the word from the Dutch, who played some comparable game (only without that essential Scottish contribution, the hole) that involved hitting a ball with a *colf* or *kolf*: Dutch for *club*. *Kolf* sounds like hitting, all right, but it's too close to *sclaff* for my comfort. Then too, *golf* introduces a strong hint of *gulp*. Not to mention the vast *gulf* between that pretty green up ahead and where you are standing.

After a number of strokes (defined by *The New Oxford American Dictionary* as "a sudden disabling attack or loss of consciousness caused by an interruption in the flow of blood to the brain"), we have reached that green. And must *putt*. Which is not, ideally, the same as punt. The roots of putt are the same as those of *put*, as in "Just put that down anywhere." *Chambers Dictionary of Etymology* says the golf term was probably associated, back around the 14th century, "with earlier *putting*, now known as *shot putting*." And indeed it may be as hard to get a

> YOU MAY HAVE ASSUMED THAT THE WORD WAS *FLOG* BACKWARDS, AS IN SELF-FLAGELLATION. BUT NO.

golf ball into a four-and-a-quarter-inch hole as to fit a sixteen-pound ball of lead into that same receptacle. But of course *putt* rhymes not with *foot* (as does *put*) but with *but*. As in, "I had the break figured perfectly, but. . . ."

Speaking of putts, and the anxiety of confronting a necessary short one, the nervous condition known as *yips* is "probably imitative of jerky motions caused by tension," says the *American Heritage Dictionary*. Tommy Armour is sometimes credited with coining the term. "Once you've had 'em, you've got 'em," he said. Yep.

Bogey is a word that managed to turn a relatively easygoing concept into a demon. In the late 1800s, holes, and courses, began to have target scores by which a player could be judged. *Par*, deriving probably from the financial term *par value*, was pretty much perfect. An unofficial, less demanding standard, which a good amateur should be able to equal, came to be called *bogey*: the bogeyman of should-be-able was breathing down the amateur's neck.

Birdie probably came from "a bird of a shot," *bird* meaning something like *hell*. An *eagle* is better than a birdie (unless it is breathing down your neck). A double eagle, three under par, is called an *albatross*, which may seem odd, since shooting that bird at sea is regarded as disastrous luck. Shooting one on a golf course just makes everyone hate you.

The origin of *tee* is a mystery. It doesn't have to do with the little wooden deal's shape, because the original tees were small mounds of sand. Dust to dust, tee to trap.

The man for whom the *mulligan* was named is identified in various stories, but none is confirmable—perhaps because, although many a *duffer* (origin also obscure) would be happy to claim the indulgence, no one ever wanted to claim the honor. It would be like saying, "You'll concede me that eight-footer, I assume, for I am the eponymous James E. Gimme."

When Mary Queen of Scots, who had grown to womanhood in France, returned to Scotland and hit the *links* (from the Scottish for "ridges, hummocks"), she called the boy who carried her clubs a *cadet*, rhyming with *paté*. Her countrymen heard it as *caddie*. The derogatory term *cad* seems to have come from *caddie*, possibly owing to the snobbish assumption that anyone who schleps things for the high and mighty is low and ill-mannered.

It isn't usually a caddie, however, who resorts to the use of a *foot wedge*: a stealthy lie-improving kick. Looking into golf terms, you might get the impression that cheating is not the only bad habit that may taint the game's venerable purity. The *19th hole*, for instance, has long been associated with strong drink. And then, let's face it, there's gambling.

The *air press* is a bet called while a ball is in the air. If your opponent's drive is headed for the rough, you can call "air press" and the bet (for a predetermined stake) must be accepted. Then if your own drive appears to be even more misdirected, your opponent can call the same thing, doubling the bet.

An *Arnie*, or a *Seve*, is a side bet won by a golfer who pars a hole without ever managing to find the fairway, in honor of those masters of the hard way, Palmer and Ballesteros.

You collect on a *barkie* when you par a hole despite hitting the trunk of a tree—leaves don't count.

Bingo Bango Bongo (first one on the green gets Bingo, and so on) is a more sophisticated game of chance, and conceivably skill, than the sort of bingo that just involves putting beans on numbered squares, and it also gets you out in the sunshine and away from church. (You can't curse in church.)

But enough of this short-hitting lexicography. You the reader undoubtedly recall the late George Plimpton's dictum that "the smaller the ball, the more formidable the literature"—that there are "not many good books about football, or soccer, very few good books about basketball, and no good books at all about beach balls," but "there are superb books about golf." So you must already be shouting *Fore!* (Which means "look out ahead." More helpful, from the standpoint of those being shouted at, would be *Aft!*, meaning "watch your back.") You're itching to read on through to bold sagas and images of robust men and women wielding *blasters* and *baffies*.

Damn. I forgot that those too, are obsolete words for approach-shot implements. Wielding *irons*, then. So cold, so clinical. As if you knew precisely what will become of the ball after you hit it with a given iron, even if you hit it right. According to Webster's Third, the word *iron* is etymologically akin to the Sanskrit for "he sets in motion, swings" and the Latin for *wrath*. There ought to be a club called the *wrathie*, especially designed for wrapping around a tree.

> OF COURSE *PUTT* RHYMES NOT WITH *FOOT* BUT WITH *BUT*. AS IN, "I HAD THE BREAK FIGURED PERFECTLY, BUT. . ."

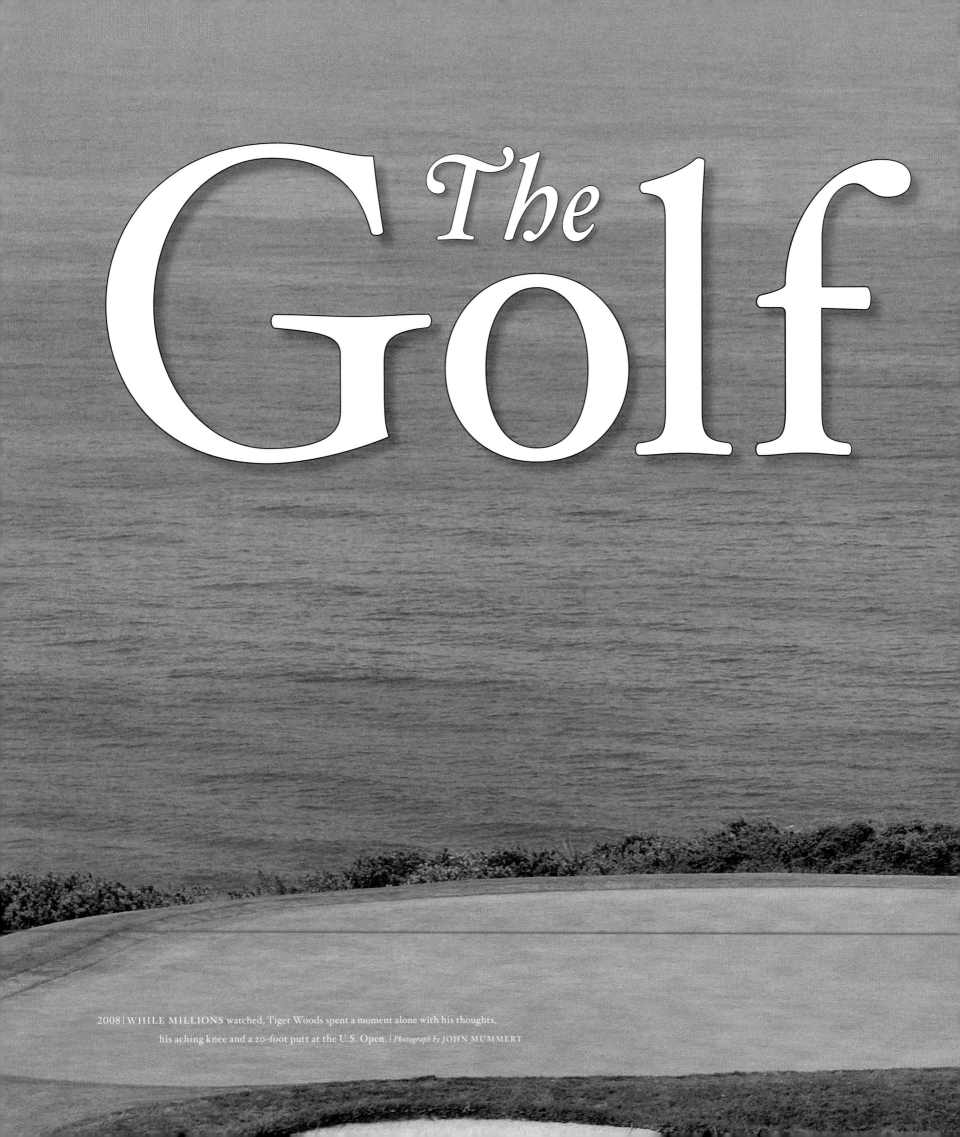

The Golf

2008 | WHILE MILLIONS watched, Tiger Woods spent a moment alone with his thoughts, his aching knee and a 20-foot putt at the U.S. Open. | *Photograph by* JOHN MUMMERT

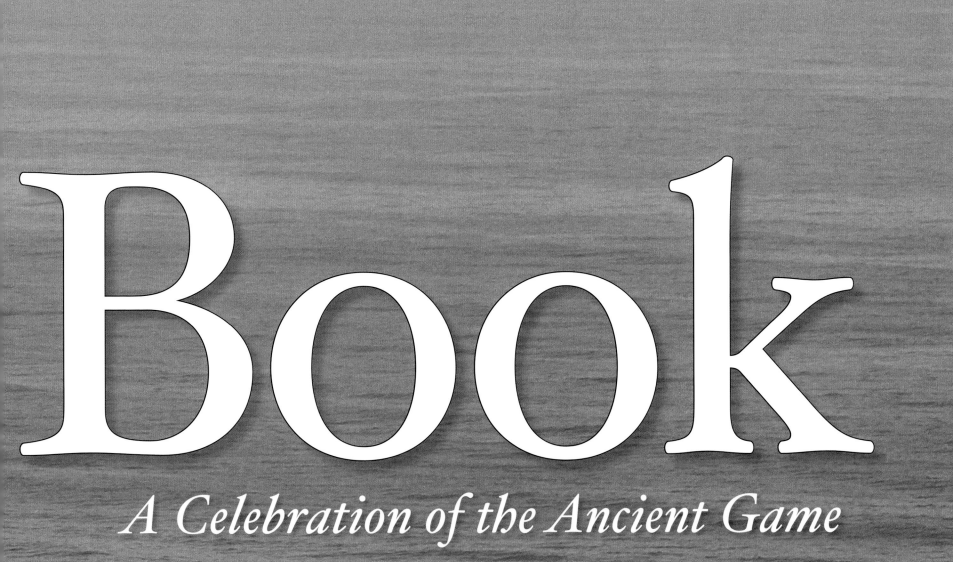

Book

A Celebration of the Ancient Game

1991 | SPAIN'S SEVE BALLESTEROS (left) and José María Olazábal were seldom shaky in the Ryder Cup, going a career 11-2-2 as Cup partners. | *Photograph by* BOB THOMAS

2004 | IN CONTRAST to his rep as a man whose swing resembled "an octopus falling out of a tree," Jim Furyk looked sharp at the end of the day. | *Photograph by* ACTION IMAGES

2005 | CAPE KIDNAPPERS in New Zealand, formerly a sheep farm, featured
460-foot cliffs and green fees that were almost as steep. | *Photograph by* DAVID CANNON

1960 | THE KING, Arnold Palmer, cavorted on the dance floor at Cherry Hills during his epic charge at the 1960 U.S. Open. | *Photograph by* JOHN G. ZIMMERMAN

2008 | THE QUEEN of the LPGA, Lorena Ochoa, stalked her realm like a tigress during a streak of five wins in six starts. | *Photograph by* MIKE EHRMANN

1457 – 1912

In the Beginning...

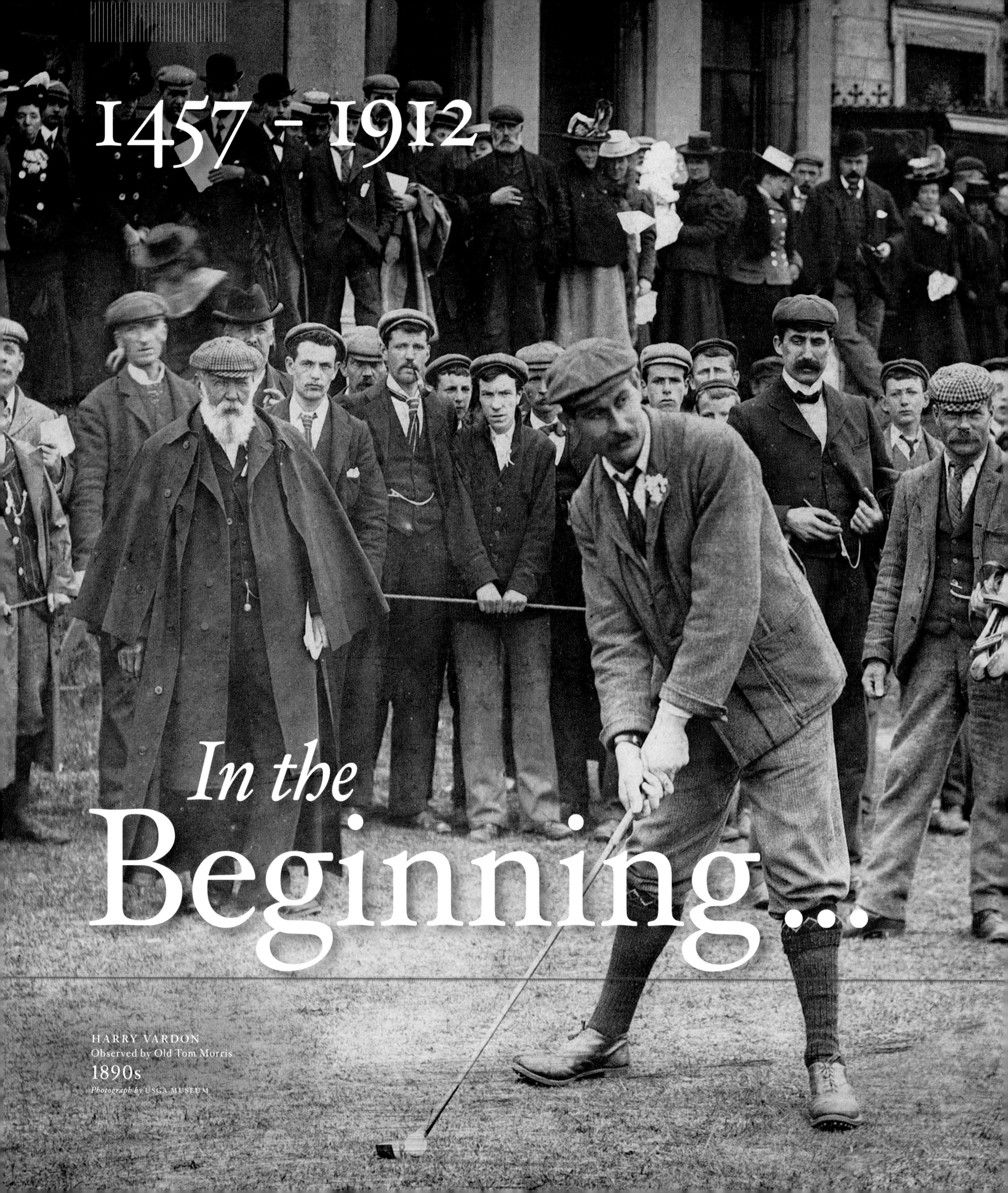

HARRY VARDON
Observed by Old Tom Morris
1890s
Photograph by USGA MUSEUM

THE ERA'S BEST

Harry Vardon

The first pro to play in knickers won the British Open six times, setting a record that still stands, and in 1900 became the first foreign-born golfer to bag a U.S. Open title.

Young Tom Morris

Strong, daring and handsome, he outdid his father by winning four straight British Opens and dominating the early professional game before his sudden death at age 24.

Old Tom Morris

Another four-time British Open victor as well as a greenkeeper, course designer and mentor to champions, he wasn't the best player but was the game's most influential figure.

J.H. Taylor

The glummest-looking golfer in any field, the five-time British Open champion explained his stoic mien by saying, "lightheartedness of endeavor is a sure sign of eventual failure."

James Braid

A member of Britain's "Great Triumvirate" with Vardon and Taylor, he won five British Opens, four British Match Play titles and a French Open, and promoted golf as a profession.

>MILESTONES<

1457
KING JAMES II OF SCOTLAND
Bans playing of "the golfe"

1557
MARY, QUEEN OF SCOTS
First known female golfer

1744
HONOURABLE COMPANY OF
EDINBURGH GOLFERS
Issues rules St. Andrews adopts

1860
FIRST BRITISH OPEN >
Old Tom Morris finishes second

1888
ST. ANDREWS IN YONKERS, N.Y.
First U.S. club founded

1894
U.S. GOLF ASSOCIATION
Formed December 22

1904
SUMMER OLYMPICS
George Lyon wins gold in golf

1904
WALTER TRAVIS
First Yank to win British Amateur

1912
BYRON NELSON
Born February 4

1912
BEN HOGAN
Born August 13

NOW OPEN FOR PLAY

The Old Course
ST. ANDREWS, SCOTLAND
15th Century / Designed by Nature
< SCULPTED OVER CENTURIES BY WIND AND WEATHER, THE
ANCIENT LINKS SET THE STANDARD FOR EVERY OTHER COURSE.

Chicago Golf Club
WHEATON, ILLINOIS
1892 / Charles Blair Macdonald

Oakmont Country Club
OAKMONT, PENNSYLVANIA
1903 / Henry Fownes

Pinehurst (No. 2)
PINEHURST, NORTH CAROLINA
1907 / Donald Ross

>> GOLF IN THE REAL WORLD <<

King James Bans the Game March 6, 1457 The first known mention of golf comes in response to a fad: Scotsmen have been playing sports instead of honing the archery skills they need to fight the English. At the behest of James II, Scotland's parliament decrees that "fut ball and golfe must be utterly cryit dune," banning soccer and golf. As late as 1491, disobeying the mandate leads to fines and prison terms for golfers as well as the lairds who own the links.

Mary Widow 1557 Like her father King James V, Mary Stuart > takes up the game at an early age. After becoming the Queen of Scots, Mary scandalizes nobles and church leaders by playing only a few days after her husband, Lord Darnley, is murdered.

A Fine Mess December 10, 1659 The village of Beverwijck (now Albany), N.Y., imposes a fine of 25 gilders for playing "kolf" in the streets. Kolfers are undeterred: The area's Dutch settlers strap on skates and take to the frozen Hudson River to play.

Bully on the Bronx 1895 The New York City Parks Department, whose commissioners include James Roosevelt—uncle of future president Theodore Roosevelt—opens the first public golf course in the U.S. Backed by local golfers known as the Riverdale Group, Van Cortlandt Park Golf Course in the Bronx gives average Americans a shot at a sport that had been the exclusive preserve of the rich. It still does: Today's weekday green fee at Van Cortlandt Park is $34.50.

Vardon Fever Grips U.S. 1900 The game's popularity grows by leaps and bounds when British golf hero Harry Vardon embarks on a whirlwind tour of America. The main purpose of his tour is to hawk the new "Vardon Flyer," a gutta-percha ball sold by Spalding that makes Vardon the first sports figure to endorse a product.

A Scotsman carried his dying partner off the course. "You kind fellow!" someone said. "The worst bit," said the golfer, "was layin' him down and pickin' him up between shots."

BEST SHOT
SEPTEMBER 14, 1868
Young Tom Morris
The Tiger Woods of the 19th century aces the 166-yard 8th hole at Prestwick during the British Open. The first recorded hole in one helps Morris, 17, become the youngest-ever major champion, a record that still stands.

WORST SHOT
JULY 31, 1888
Freddie Tait
During a match at St. Andrews, the future British Amateur champion smacks a drive that hits a spectator and destroys his hat. Old Tom Morris makes Tait pay the fan five shillings, saying, "Be thankful 'tis a hat and no' an oak coffin ye have to pay for."

> THE SWING

Harry Vardon, *encumbered by a tweed jacket, took the club back inside the target line and had a "soft" left arm throughout.*

> GOLF EVOLVES

THE FIRST CLUBHOUSE The Golf House at Leith Links, built in 1768 by the Honourable Company of Edinburgh Golfers, provides refuge at the club that also hosted the first known tournament, in 1744.

STROKE PLAY Without time for a match-play round-robin, club officials at St. Andrews stage a 1759 event in which the low score wins. The stroke-play format is born.

THE 18-HOLE ROUND In 1764 the Society of St. Andrews Golfers defines a round of golf as 18 holes, the standard at the Society's home course, the Old Course.

LAWN MOWERS Grazing sheep are the only form of course maintenance for centuries, but in 1830 the first patent for a lawn mower goes to British engineer Edwin Beard Budding. For the first time, the game can move inland from seaside links.

DIMPLES Inventor William Taylor discovers that balls covered with dents fly higher and farther than "bramble" balls with bumps. The "Dympl" debuts in 1905.

GAME CHANGER: HOLE CUTTERS
First employed at Musselburgh Golf Club in Scotland in 1829, the original hole cutter (*above*) was 4¼" across, matching local drainpipes used as cup-liners. In 1891 the R&A makes 4¼" the hole's official diameter.

>> FROM THE VAULT

"When Harry Vardon first visited our country at the turn of the century, his accuracy was so confounding that it nurtured the famous mythological story that Harry never liked to play a course twice the same day: On his afternoon round he had to play out of the divot marks he had made that morning."

—Herbert Warren Wind *in* SI, June 10, 1957

> ON THE NUMBER

2 Charles Blair Macdonald's finish in the first two U.S. golf championships, held in 1894. So incensed was runner-up C.B. that he helped found the USGA—which declared the '94 events unofficial—and won the 1895 U.S. Amateur.

$100 Original 1891 cost to join Shinnecock Hills, the first incorporated golf club in the nation. Membership today—if you're invited—costs more than $500,000.

5 Strokes frittered away by Alex Smith, who led the 1901 U.S. Open by five with five holes to play. Two double-bogeys, two bogeys and a par dropped Smith into a playoff he lost to Willie Anderson.

5 Wimbledon Ladies Singles tennis titles for Lottie Dod, the 1904 British Amateur Ladies Golf champion, making her the only woman ever to capture both crowns.

13 Rules drafted by the Honourable Company of Edinburgh Golfers in 1744—the template used by the Society of St. Andrews Golfers a decade later.

69 Score in the third round of the 1904 British Open by James Braid, the first tournament player to break 70 over 18 holes.

16 Courses in the United States in 1893, a number that would balloon to more than 1,000 by 1900.

1953 | AT CARNOUSTIE, where the tightly wound Ben Hogan won the claret jug in his only
British Open appearance, adoring Scots dubbed him "the Wee Ice Mon." | *Photograph by* BETTMANN

1940s | EYEBALLING HIS line suited Sam Snead in the years before the yips led him to try putting croquet-style. | *Photograph by* AUGUSTA NATIONAL

2006 | FASHION, FITNESS and a flashy way of lining up putts made golf's Spider-Man, Camilo Villegas, a sensation on Tour. | *Photograph by* DAVID WALBERG

GOLF'S GREATEST PUTT

BY GRANTLAND RICE

In the first SPORTS ILLUSTRATED golf story, one immortal hailed another. Rice died less than a month before this piece appeared in the magazine's inaugural issue. —*from* SI, AUGUST 16, 1954

O N A LATE JUNE AFTERNOON in 1929, some 10,000 tense spectators crowded up to the 18th green at the Winged Foot Golf Club in Westchester County, New York. As they came running up to the green, crowding as close as they could get, you heard every type of sound from a whisper to a shriek blended into one vast babble of excited human voices. The startling news was passed from person to person—Bob Jones was on the verge of the worst catastrophe any U.S. Open had ever known.

As Jones broke through the crowd and came upon the green, the babble suddenly was stilled. This was the silence of suppressed nerves. Since the first Scottish herdsman addressed an early golf ball with a shepherd's crook, I doubt if any golfer had ever faced a moment so packed with tension.

It was one of the great moments I have ever known in sports. The silence was complete. Only a few short minutes before, Jones had been six strokes up with only six holes to go. Now he had one putt left, for a tie. Bobby Jones had faced crucial putts before—more of them than any other golfer I have ever known—where important championships were at stake. But this putt meant more to Bob Jones than merely winning an Open. It meant the recapture of his golfing soul. It meant removing a dark stain from his pride, certain nationwide ridicule that would follow failure.

Let's go back a minute. The real drama of this, the 33rd Open, and of Bob Jones's career, started at the long 12th hole.

Here Al Espinosa, the only challenger, took a destructive 8. When Espinosa took this 8, he felt he had no chance. With the tension off, he finished with four 4s and two 3s for a 75 and a total of 294.

Even with this spurt on Espinosa's part, Jones could drop three strokes to par over the last six holes and still win. There never was a surer thing in golf.

Bob lost one stroke at the short 13, and then at the 15th he had a heartbreaking 7, three over par. Now he needed three pars to tie Espinosa. Here was undoubtedly the finest golfer in the world...yet no duffer had ever blown so bad.

Jones got his pars on 16 and 17 and came to the final hole needing a par 4 to tie his Mexican-American rival. Bob's drive was good. His second shot hit the hard, keen green and ran down a grassy bank. He chipped from below, but the chip stopped 12 to 14 feet short. He stopped as he came up on the green and saw how far short he was—the putt he had to hole to even get a draw.

This wasn't the first 10- or 12- foot putt Bob had had to sink in his brilliant career...I could name any number of 10-footers he had holed to keep from being beaten on some closing green. I might add here that over a long period of years I have seen five great putters—Walter Travis, Jerry Travers, Walter Hagen, Horton Smith and Bobby Jones. I believe Jones was the greatest for the simple reason that he saved himself more times by holing the important ones—the 8- and 10-footers against George Voigt, against Cyril Tolley, against Maurice McCarthy, to beat out Gene Sarazen and Hagen in so many championships here and abroad.

But this occasion at Winged Foot was different. Jones's competitive career, by his own choice, was nearing its end. He had been working seriously at the game since he was seven years old. He was now 27. The 1929 title meant his third U.S. Open. He had finished one-two in this Open since '22, eight years with only one exception—'27. Later O.B. Keeler, Jones's Boswell and the best golf writer this country ever produced, told me that if Bob had missed this putt he would never have gone abroad the next year to make his Grand Slam.

On the green Bobby Jones crouched partly on one knee studying the slanting line of the treacherous putt. There was a dip or a break in the green of at least a foot-and-a-half that had to be judged. Bob was usually a fast putter. This time he took a few seconds longer than usual, for in addition to the speed of the fast green he had to decide how big the break was.

I was with Mike Brady, the club pro, when the putt was made. I was on the ground, peering between legs. Mike had a stepladder and was above the mob.

"He's short," Mike shouted. "He's missed it. He's short." I lost the ball en route. I picked it up again near the cup. Suddenly the ball hesitated, stopped—and then turned over once more and disappeared. . . .

WITH THE OPEN on the line at Winged Foot, Jones drew back his putter, Calamity Jane, and sent a sidehill 12-footer toward the cup.

1977 | AFTER HIS epic Duel in the Sun with Jack Nicklaus, victorious Tom Watson basked in the crowd's adulation. | *Photograph by* STEPHEN GREEN-ARMYTAGE

2005 | POPULAR PHIL MICKELSON won his second major at the PGA Championship, then pressed the flesh with kids eager to get their Phil. | *Photograph by* ROBERT BECK

1839 | A "FEATHERY" made by Allan Robertson, the first golf professional, who crafted balls the old-fashioned way:

by stuffing boiled goose feathers into a leather pouch he sewed shut with waxed thread. | *Photograph by* DAVID N. BERKWITZ

> **Artifacts**

Sphere Factors

Made of feathers, rubber or high-tech plastics, the ball's fundamental however you slice it

1840s
Unplayed Robertson feathery

1860s
"Gutty" of gutta-percha tree sap

1890s
Red gutty for winter play

1897
First ball patented in America

1900
Rubber "Haskell bramble"

c. 1908
Commemorative globe bramble

c. 1912
Crescent-dimpled rubber ball

1914
Diamond-dimpled rubber

1916
Chick Evans's U.S. Open winner

c. 1930
Rubber-cored yellow "Tiger"

c. 1958
Eisenhower's personal balata ball

2000
Tiger Woods's brand

2000 | MARK O'MEARA left his imprint on the game by winning two majors, mentoring a young

Tiger Woods and denting the bunker with this rim shot during the Masters. | *Photograph by* JOHN BIEVER

THE COURSE: MAGIC AND MYSTERY

BY S.L. McKINLAY

At a time when few American golfers made pilgrimages to the game's ancestral home, Scottish writer McKinlay offered a guide to the Old Course at St. Andrews. —*from* SI, JULY 1, 1957

WITHOUT DOUBT, THE right way to approach St. Andrews is by train; and the right way to approach the Old Course is on foot by a route I shall prescribe. This is necessary because there are two moments of magic that any golfer of sensibility may savor at St. Andrews if he takes the wise precaution. Other wonderful moments there will be, too—as when he gets his first 4 at the Road Hole, or sends a second shot triumphantly over Hell Bunker, or is taken into the holy of holies, the back room of Laurie Auchterlonie's little shop, and sees one of the few remaining craftsmen fashioning with his enormous hands a wooden clubhead that may be destined for the bag of an Amateur champion or for a British proconsul in some remote pink area on the map of the world.

Those later moments may be the result of luck or skillful contriving. The two that may be captured by every new visitor to the old gray town, which is the heart and head of golf, are these: his first sight of St. Andrews hanging on its clifftop over the sea and the links, and his first sight of the Old Course lying at his feet.

To begin with, the intelligent visitor must go by train, any train that drops him at Leuchars Junction, where he picks up a little local train that will take him the few miles to St. Andrews. The fussy little train puffs on in a wide curve, and there, lying straight ahead, is one of the most beautiful skylines in the golfer's world—an old castle, lofty towers of a medieval cathedral, tall tenements, the St. Andrews University buildings and an isolated block of red sandstone in the otherwise uniform gray, what is still known as the Grand Hotel though it is now a students' hostel.

The golfer may do with his gear as he wishes, but I insist that he now take a walk of a few hundred yards and have a look at the course he has come to play. He will find himself in a pleasant town with many trees. A few minutes' walk will bring him to Pilmuir Links and, passing Laurie Auchterlonie's shop on his left hand, he will come to a narrow street called Golf Place, which runs off to the left.

In the distance he will catch a glimpse of the sea. Let him walk a bare 50 yards and there, virtually at his feet, lies the Tom Morris green, the 18th on the Old Course, right under the shadow of the hotels, golf shops and golf clubhouses that line the last fairway for three quarters of its length.

Inevitably someone will be playing the last hole, be the hour mid-morning or late evening; equally inevitably, a group of onlookers will be lining the fence at the back of the green, nodding sagely as some player fails, again inevitably, to judge the borrow on his putt. Someone, too, will be driving from the 1st tee, and someone will certainly be standing at the window of the Great Room of the Royal and Ancient clubhouse, keeping one eye on the drive, the other on the players on the last green.

Our newcomer will not see all this at first glance; the moment of magic may be a bit overwhelming. Indeed, he may not think it is a moment of magic at all, because when he lifts his eyes beyond the home green he will see what appears to be only a rectangular field about 300 yards long by 80 or 90 yards wide, bisected by a road along which motorcars are rolling, mothers are pushing perambulators and riding-school ponies are trotting. Yet this bisected field comprises the first and last fairways of the most famous golf course in the world—not a bunker, not a bush, not a tree, nothing.

To the American accustomed to seeing courses neatly tailored and trapped according to the best standards laid down by the strategists, this flat, wide-open space can be perplexing and sadly disappointing. This perplexity will increase when he plays his first round on the Old Course. He hits a beauty on a distant flag—and finds his ball trapped; trapped, moreover, in a bunker that he could not see from the tee. If he escapes the bunkers, seen and unseen, he may find his ball lying either perched on a little knoll or tucked in a little hollow. The lie may be bare or lush, his stance crooked or normal. His target will more often than not be a naked flagstick, either on a skyline or behind a ridge or mound.

Mystery is everywhere, and perhaps it is this that gives St. Andrews golf its essential flavor. Nothing is cut-and-dried, straightforward, made-to-measure, not even the greens. All the world knows that St. Andrews' greens are the biggest in golf. . . .

THE OPENING hole plays outward from the Royal and Ancient clubhouse; the last leads golfers over trundling turf to the home green, just past the Valley of Sin.

2008 | CARLY BOOTH of Great Britain & Ireland (right) coaxed a putt cupward while Curtis Cup teammate Breanne Loucks sympathized. | *Photograph by* MATTHEW HARRIS

1964 | THE GREAT ONE himself, heavy hitter Jackie Gleason, made ready to exit stage left with his trademark "And . . . *awayyy we go.*" | *Photograph by* BOB EAST

1995 | NICK FALDO and his caddie Fanny Sunesson, one of the few female loopers
on the pro circuit, both fell behind at the British Open. | *Photograph by* BOB MARTIN

THE FATEFUL CORNER

BY HERBERT WARREN WIND

Wind has always been a factor in Amen Corner, the pivotal stretch of holes that Herbert Warren Wind named in his report on the controversial 1958 Masters.   —*from* SI, APRIL 21, 1958

ON THE AFTERNOON BEFORE the start of the recent Masters golf tournament, a wonderfully evocative ceremony took place at the farthest reach of the Augusta National course—down in the Amen Corner where Rae's Creek intersects the 13th fairway near the tee, then parallels the front edge of the green on the short 12th and finally swirls alongside the 11th green. On that afternoon, with Bob Jones investing the occasion with his invariable flavor, two new bridges across the creek were officially dedicated. one (leading to the 12th green) to Ben Hogan, commemorat-

ing his record score of 274 in the 1953 tournament; the other (leading back to the fairway from the 13th tee) to Byron Nelson, commemorating his great burst in the '37 Masters when, trailing Ralph Guldahl by four strokes on the last round, he played a birdie 2 on the 12th and an eagle 3 on the 13th, made up six strokes on Guldahl (who had taken a 5 and a 6 on these holes) and rolled on to victory. While Nelson's exploit is certainly the most striking illustration of what can happen at this particular bend of the course, history has had a way of affixing itself to these two holes.

On the final round, the new champion, Arnold Palmer, the co-leader with Sam Snead at the end of the first three rounds, was paired with the bona-fide sensation, Ken Venturi. The two young men were the first contenders to go out, which is important to keep in mind. By the time Palmer and Venturi came to the 12th hole it seemed fairly certain that the winner of their duel might well turn out to be the winner of

AUTHOR WIND watched Palmer's tee shot plug in wet turf behind the 12th green, leading the future King to make both a 3 and a 5 on the hole.

the tournament. Venturi had cut one stroke off of Palmer's three-stroke lead by going out in 35 and had cut a second shot off it on the 10th. With seven holes to go, then, only one shot separated them.

The 12th at the Augusta National, 155 yards long, can be a very delicate and dangerous affair when the pin is placed at the far righthand corner of the green (which it was) and when there is a puffy wind to contend with (which there was). You've got to be up, over Rae's Creek—that's for sure. But you can't take too much club, because the green is extremely thin and on the far side a high bank of rough rises abruptly behind the apron—and you don't want to be there either. Venturi and Palmer both hit their tee shots over the green and into the bank. Venturi's ball kicked down onto the far side of the green, presenting him with a probable 3 (which he went on to make). Palmer's ball struck low on the bank about a foot or so below the bottom rim of a bankside trap and embedded itself. It had rained heavily during the night and early morning, and parts of the course were soggy.

Now the drama began to unfold, and because of the unusual setting it was indeed charged with the quality of theater: Only the players, their caddies and officials are allowed beyond the roping around the 12th tee, and one could only watch the pantomime activity taking place on the distant stage of the 12th green and try to decipher what was happening. To begin with, there was an animated and protracted discussion between

Palmer and a member of the tournament's rules committee, obviously on the subject as to whether or not Palmer could lift his ball without penalty. Apparently the official had decided he couldn't, for Arnold at length addressed the half-buried ball and budged it about a foot and a half with his wedge. It ended up in casual water then, so he lifted and dropped it (patently without penalty) and then chipped close to the pin on his third stroke. He missed the putt and took a 5. This put him a stroke behind Venturi.

Then the situation became really confusing. Palmer did not walk off the green and head for the 13th tee. He returned to the spot in the rough just behind the apron where his ball had been embedded and, with the member of the rules committee standing by, dropped the ball over his shoulder. It rolled down the slope a little, so he placed the ball near the pit-mark. Apparently, now, the official had not been sure of what ruling to make and Palmer was playing a provisional or alternate ball in the event it might later be decided he had a right to lift and drop without penalty. He chipped stone-dead again and this time holed the putt for a 3. Now the question was: Was Palmer's score a 3 or a 5? . . .

The rules of golf are very touchy and troublous things to administer, and my own feeling on the subject is that if a man is notified he has been appointed to serve on the rules committee he should instantly remember that he must attend an important business meeting in Khartoum. . . .

Silver Scot's Sweet Spot

Tommy Armour of Edinburgh, golf's famed Silver Scot, hit the ball on the screws of this driver. "L.F.F." was short for his motto, "Let the f---er fly"

1921 | AMATEUR CHAMPION Armour went on to win three pro majors, mentor Babe Didrikson Zaharias and blaze a trail for his grandson, Tour standout Tommy Armour III.

1993 | GARY PLAYER'S ball reached escape velocity as he launched it from the U.K.'s deepest bunker during the British Open. | *Photograph by* JACQUELINE DUVOISIN

2007 | GRITTY ZACH JOHNSON made a face while awaiting a face full of Florida blowback at the PODS Championship. | *Photograph by* CHRIS O'MEARA

2006 | PAULA CREAMER kept her head down and followed through with an LPGA title before she turned 19. | *Photograph by* PHILIPPE MILLEREAU

2003 | A PUMPED-UP Annika Sorenstam settled for second place at the Kraft Nabisco, but won six times the rest of the year. | *Photograph by* ROBERT BECK

AMEN

BY ALAN SHIPNUCK

Before, Phil Mickelson was everybody's favorite underachiever, the Best Player Never to Have Won a Major. After, he was something far more masterly, with a green jacket to prove it.
—*from* SI, APRIL 19, 2004

LATE ON EASTER SUNDAY, PHIL Mickelson stood over a birdie putt on the 18th hole to win the 68th Masters, and it was as quiet as church. Thousands of fans had encircled the green, glowing from sweat and the most exciting Masters finish since 46-year-old Jack Nicklaus reinvented himself in 1986. Ernie Els, the game's gentle giant, was in the clubhouse after a dazzling 67, having rushed to the lead of the tournament with two eagles in a span of six holes midway through the round. Mickelson had chased him down with a back-nine charge for the ages, and now, having endured countless heartbreaks in his decade-plus pursuit of a first major championship, Mickelson was facing the most important putt of his career, 18 feet that meant so much to so many.

Behind the green was Mickelson's wife and college sweetheart, Amy. She had been blinking back tears since the 15th hole, so overwhelming was the emotion of the day. Nearby two sets of grandparents were passing around Phil and Amy's three young children, including Evan, who had just turned a year old. In March 2003 Amy and Evan had both nearly died during childbirth. Phil was so shaken by the trauma that he sleepwalked through the 2003 season, his worst in 12 years on the PGA Tour.

In San Diego, Mickelson's 92-year-old grandmother, Jennie Santos, was resting comfortably in front of the TV. She had been getting ready to leave for Augusta when she suffered a mild stroke. Just before Christmas, Jennie's husband, Al, had died at 97. He had adorned their kitchen with the 18th-hole flags from each of their grandson's first 21 wins on Tour. Finally, in 2002, he told Phil that the only flag he would accept was one from a major championship. Shortly before his death Al whispered to Phil that this would be the year he broke through.

All of this feeling and personal history was distilled into one downhill, right-to-left putt. At last Mickelson nudged his ball toward the cup. He had been on the other end of one of these life-changing strokes, Payne Stewart's 18-footer for par on the final hole of the 1999 U.S. Open at Pinehurst. At that moment Amy was in Scottsdale, Ariz., trying to slow the signs of labor, as their first child, Amanda, was on the way. When the putt dropped, dealing Mickelson another in a string of devastating defeats, Stewart took Mickelson's face in his hands and told him that becoming a major champion could not compare to becoming a father. Now, five years later at Augusta National, Mickelson was on the verge of being both.

The putt crawled toward the hole. Moments earlier Mickelson had studied playing partner Chris DiMarco's unsuccessful effort from virtually the same spot. "Chris's ball was hanging on that left lip, and when it got to the hole, it just fell off," Mickelson said. "And my putt was almost on the identical line. Instead of falling off, it caught that lip and circled around and went in. I can't help but think [my grandfather] may have had a little something to do with that."

The crowd exploded, a release years in the making. Mickelson did a low-flying jumping jack and screamed, "I did it!" His longtime caddie, Jim (Bones) Mackay, rushed over for a hug. Mickelson walked behind the green and scooped up his daughter Sophia. "Daddy won! Can you believe it?" he said.

He wrapped Amy in a long, tearful hug. The 18th green at the Masters has seen some of golf's most memorable displays of emotion. Phil and Amy were in almost the same spot where Tiger Woods and his father, Earl, embraced after Tiger's victory in 1997. The final green is where Ben Crenshaw was doubled over in agony and ecstasy after having been guided to victory in '95 by the unseen hand of his teacher Harvey Penick, who died two days before the tournament began.

Now Mickelson had joined the pantheon of Masters winners. After 17 career top 10s in the majors, including three straight third-place finishes at Augusta, he had proved himself in the most audacious fashion imaginable. On a course that is far tougher than it was in '86, when Nicklaus shot a back-nine 30 to surge to victory, Mickelson birdied five of the last seven holes to finish with a 31 on the final nine on Sunday. He became only the sixth player to win the Masters with a birdie on the 72nd hole, a list that includes Arnold Palmer, who had a birdie-birdie finish in 1960.

"Now we can finally stamp him APPROVED," said Davis Love III, a close friend of Mickelson's. "It's like a...what's the right word?...It's like a coronation."...

AFTER 12 YEARS as a pro and 46 majors without a victory, Mickelson turned his clinching putt into golf's most famous jump shot.

1969 | TONY JACKLIN missed this putt in the Ryder Cup matches that ended when Jack Nicklaus, in an act of supreme sportsmanship, conceded a shorter one to halve the event, leaving the Cup in American hands. | *Photograph by* GERRY CRANHAM

1960 | AFTER SPLASHING two tee shots at the U.S. Open, Tommy "Thunder" Bolt, lying 4, heaved his driver into the drink. | *Photograph by* JOHN G. ZIMMERMAN

1999 | FRANK LICKLITER butchered a hole at the Houston Open and battered his bag, which had been lying down on the job. | *Photograph by* DARREN CARROLL

1989 | SHADOW CREEK, built on lunar desert near Las Vegas, was the $47-million brainchild of owner
Steve Wynn and designer Tom Fazio, who said he could build a course on the moon. | *Photograph by* GREG CAVA

1913 - 1930

The Golden Age

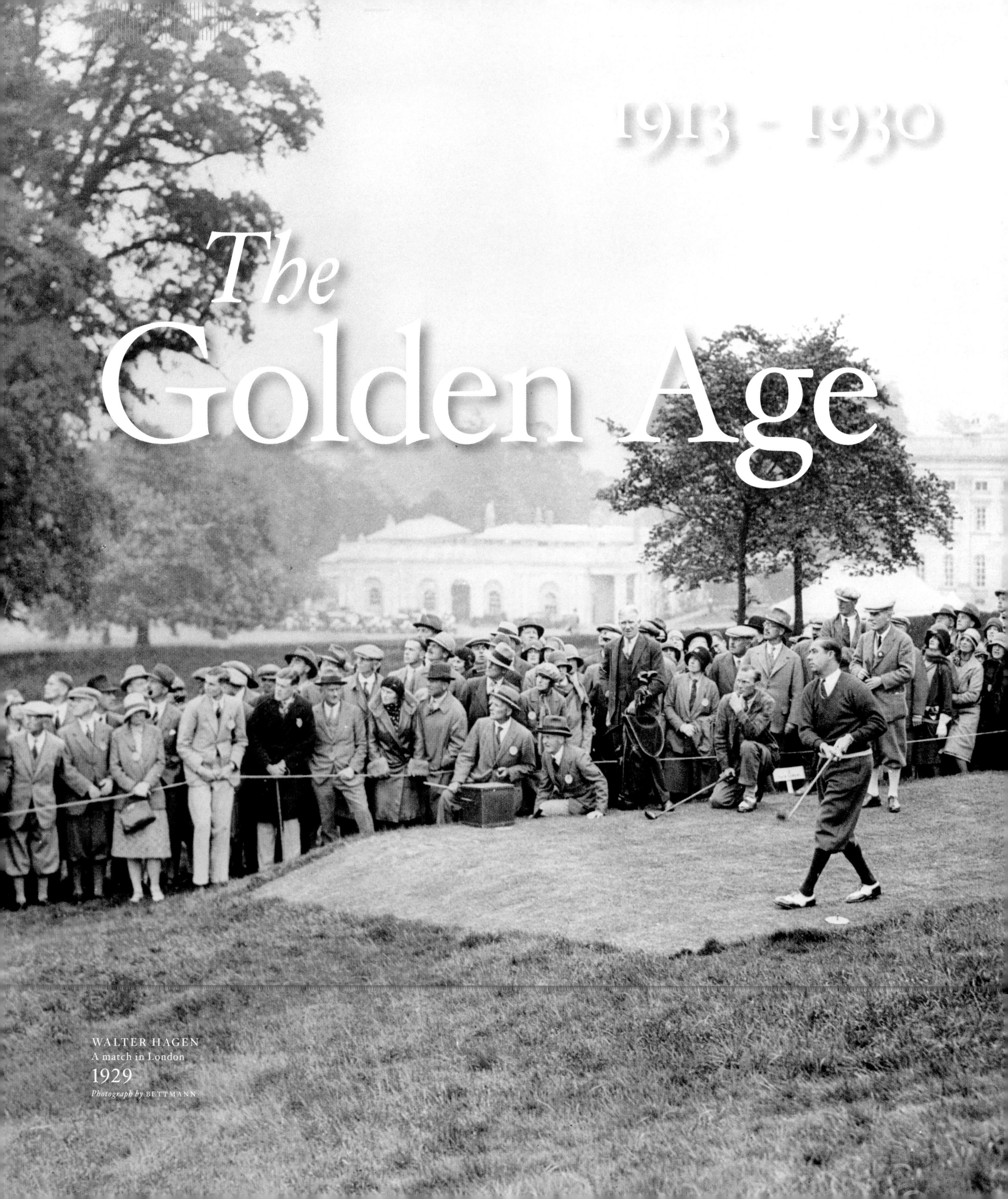

WALTER HAGEN
A match in London
1929
Photograph by BETTMANN

THE ERA'S BEST

Bobby Jones

The beloved amateur from Atlanta was highly educated, often emotional and virtually unstoppable, winning 13 of the 20 major tournaments he entered before he retired at 28.

Walter Hagen

America's first full-time touring professional, the Haig was the finest match-play golfer of his or any era, victorious in all but one of the 33 matches he played between 1921 and '28.

Gene Sarazen

Beginning with the 1922 U.S. Open, the diminutive (5' 5") sixth-grade dropout netted seven majors and became the first to win all four of the modern Grand Slam events.

Glenna Collett Vare

"The Queen of American Golf" won six Women's Amateurs and in 1924 went 59–1 in match play, her only loss coming when her opponent's ball bounced off hers and into the cup.

Tommy Armour

The Silver Scot displayed what he called "the essential quality of making very few bad shots" in becoming the third golfer to win the PGA Championship, the British Open and U.S. Open.

>MILESTONES<

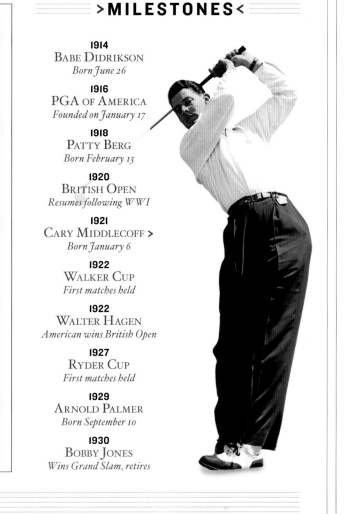

1914
BABE DIDRIKSON
Born June 26

1916
PGA OF AMERICA
Founded on January 17

1918
PATTY BERG
Born February 13

1920
BRITISH OPEN
Resumes following WWI

1921
CARY MIDDLECOFF >
Born January 6

1922
WALKER CUP
First matches held

1922
WALTER HAGEN
American wins British Open

1927
RYDER CUP
First matches held

1929
ARNOLD PALMER
Born September 10

1930
BOBBY JONES
Wins Grand Slam, retires

NOW OPEN FOR PLAY

Pebble Beach
PEBBLE BEACH, CALIFORNIA
1919 / Designed by Jack Neville & Douglas Grant

< YARD FOR YARD, FEW HOLES MATCH PEBBLE'S 110-YARD
7TH FOR BEAUTY, DRAMA OR DEVILISH DIFFICULTY.

Pine Valley
PINE VALLEY, NEW JERSEY
1918 / George Crump & H.S. Colt

Cypress Point
PEBBLE BEACH, CALIFORNIA
1928 / Alister MacKenzie

Seminole
NORTH PALM BEACH, FLORIDA
1929 / Donald Ross

>> GOLF IN THE REAL WORLD <<

Clowning a Round 1916 The first miniature golf course in America, Thistle Dhu (pronounced *this'll do*), is founded by steamship magnate James Barber in Pinehurst, N.C. By the 21st century Americans will play more than half a billion rounds of Putt-Putt, Goofy Golf, Wacky Golf and other forms of minigolf every year.

Bronx Bomber May 14, 1920 The biggest celebrity of his time, > Babe Ruth is an avid golfer who would play even on game days. One of Ruth's most satisfying days on the links is a match in which he challenges Yankees teammate Bob Shawkey and sportswriting legend Grantland Rice. Ruth chooses Metropolitan amateur champion Oswald Kirkby as his partner and despite the Bambino's 98, the foursome's worst score, his side prevails 2 and 1.

Signing the Squire 1922 Wilson Sporting Goods inks a deal with 20-year-old Gene Sarazen, who had changed his name from Saraceni the year before, as the first member of its Pro Advisory Staff. The Squire continues to pitch Wilson products until his death in '99, as his part of what is thought to be the longest-running endorsement deal in sports history.

Once Known as a Polo Shirt September 18, 1926 The now-ubiquitous golf shirt, a mainstay of Casual Fridays nationwide, is introduced by French tennis player René Lacoste, who fashions a short-sleeved, collared shirt made of jersey cloth and wears it at the U.S. Open tennis tournament. Lacoste goes on to win the Open in a final against Jean Borotra, who sports a long-sleeved dress shirt.

Time to Reload February 14, 1929 Eighties-shooter Al Capone is a regular at the Burnham Woods Golf Course just south of Chicago. According to his henchman Sam "Golf Bag" Hunt, the course is also the burial site for police uniforms, shotguns and Thompson submachine guns used in the St. Valentine's Day Massacre.

"You must be the worst caddie in the world," raged the angry golfer. "Oh, no, sir," his caddie said. "That would be too much of a coincidence."

BEST SHOT

JULY 15, 1923

Bobby Jones

In a U.S. Open playoff with Bobby Cruickshank at Inwood (N.Y.) Country Club, Jones blasts a 190-yard two-iron from the rough on his 2nd shot. The ball stops six feet from the cup and Jones earns his first major title.

WORST SHOT

JUNE 23, 1928

Roland Hancock

Leading the U.S. Open at Olympia Fields with two holes left, Hancock chunks his 2nd on the par-4 17th, advancing it just 15 feet. His double-bogey, bogey finish keeps him out of a playoff with Bobby Jones and eventual champ Johnny Farrell.

> THE SWING *To generate power* BOBBY JONES *lifted his left heel, shifted his weight forward and snapped his wrists at impact.*

> GOLF EVOLVES

THE REDDY TEE New Jersey dentist William Lowell introduces the wooden precursor of today's tee, featuring a cupped top and pointed tip, in 1922. Cheap and easy to produce, the Reddy Tee dominates the market after the inventor pays Walter Hagen to endorse it at golf shows.

A FAULTLESS BALL Thomas Miller of the Faultless Rubber Company patents a one-piece golf ball in 1923.

WATERING HOLES In 1925 Dallas's Brook Hollow Golf Club unveils the world's first tee-to-green fairway irrigation system, which feeds water through a centralized, motorized pumping station to underground pipes and hand-operated sprayers.

"PERFECT" GRASS The U.S. Department of Agriculture introduces a new species, *Agrostis stolonifera*, in 1927. Commonly called bentgrass, the "perfect putting surface" features flat blades.

GAME CHANGER: STEEL SHAFTS
Debuting in prototype form around 1910, metal shafts let golfers like Byron Nelson swing harder than they could using hickory, with less torque. The USGA legalizes them in 1926, spelling doom for old hickory.

>> FROM THE VAULT

"I STARTED IN THE 1921 Open Championship with two fair rounds. In the third round I put my tee shot into the Hill Bunker at the 11th. It is not true, as a guidebook to St. Andrews says, that I played two shots in the bunker and then knocked my ball into the Eden River. The ball came out of that bunker in my pocket, and it was my scorecard that went into the river." — BOBBY JONES *in* SI, NOVEMBER 7, 1960

> ON THE NUMBER

$1 Cost of a ticket to the 1922 U.S. Open, the first time tickets were sold for the event.

2 Presidents of the U.S.— George H.W. Bush and George W. Bush—descended from USGA president George Herbert Walker, who founded the Walker Cup in 1922.

2 Years the U.S. Open and PGA Championship were canceled due to World War I (1917, '18).

90 Courses designed by A.W. Tillinghast, one of the best and most prolific Golden Age architects, whose designs include the East and West Courses at Winged Foot, and all 36 holes at Baltusrol.

19 Putts in 18 holes during a 1926 round at Augusta Country Club by amateur champion Dorothy Campbell Hurd. The previous record was 21 by Walter Travis. (The current record, 18, is shared by six players.)

289 Yardage of the winning drive at the Pacific Coast Long Drive Championships of 1928, by Indiana's Leonard Schmutte. He also clouted bombs of 272 and 275 yards.

$500 Jim Barnes's prize money for capturing the first PGA Championship, in 1916.

1998 | GRACE PARK dominated the U.S. Women's Amateur and followed through by sweeping every major amateur event, a feat unmatched since 1938. | *Photograph by* DAVID WALBERG

2001 | THREE DECADES after he and Ben Crenshaw led Texas to the NCAA title, Tom Kite faced his old teammate on the Champions tour. | *Photograph by* ROBERT BECK

2008 | THE JEWEL of Spanish golf, Valderrama hosted the European Tour's Volvo Masters until 2008 as well as the 1997 Ryder Cup. | *Photograph by* ROSS KINNAIRD

A GAME FOR EVERY GENERATION

BY ROBERT TYRE JONES JR.

In addition to being the best golfer of his time, the Harvard-educated Robert Tyre "Bobby" Jones was an accomplished writer, as he proved in our pages. —*from* SI, NOVEMBER 7, 1960

THE ONE QUESTION STILL PUT to me most often is: "Were the golfers of your day as good as those of the present time?" No question is more difficult to answer. It is human, I suppose, for every man to think that his days were the best. Yet in 1927, when I won the British Open at St. Andrews, one of the old-time professionals, described as "the grand old man of Scottish golf," was quoted in the newspapers as follows:

"I knew and played with Tom Morris, and he was every bit as good as Jones. Young Tom had to play with a gutty ball, and you could not make a mistake and get away with it. This rubber-cored ball we have now only requires a tap and it runs a mile."

So, you see, the controversy is not new. Young Tom had died almost 30 years before I was born.

I think we must agree that all a man can do is beat the people who are around at the same time he is. He cannot win from those who came before any more than he can from those who come afterward. It is grossly unfair to anyone who takes pride in his record to see it compared to those of other players who have been competing in some different period against entirely different people under wholly different conditions.

The first thing to point out is that there is nothing absolute about scoring in golf. We all know that the same golf course can change, even from day to day, depending upon weather conditions. Furthermore, over the longer range there has been a steady improvement in the conditioning of our better golf courses. Artificial watering has led to a greater consistency in the turf of fairways and greens, weed control has given us the means of eradicating clover, crabgrass and a good many other golf course pests which often prevented the clean contact between club and ball so vital to control of iron shots.

On a properly conditioned course today, it is almost impossible to get a bad lie.

The ball, of course, has been consistently improved. Perhaps the greatest progress has been made in producing balls of greater uniformity. When you consider that a difference of five yards in the driving power of two different balls may make the difference between having a putt for a birdie and playing the next shot out of a bunker, the importance of this may be appreciated. As for the clubs, when I look today at my old clubs—clubs in which I took great pride, which had been handmade to my specifications and often under my own watchful eye—and compare them with modern clubs, I wonder why I was so proud of them.

The big difference, of course, is the steel shaft, which was just beginning to gain acceptance at the time I quit competition. A hickory shaft such as I used, of average length, say for a two-iron, would weigh a little bit over seven ounces. The same shaft in steel will weigh 4¼ to 4½ ounces. The lighter steel shaft not only provides for better balance, but it is also more resistant to the twisting stresses against which the player always has to be on guard.

Players of my era often comment that the players of today seem to hit the ball harder. They do. I think it is fair to say that players of my day hit the ball really hard only when there was something definite to be gained by doing so. On holes of the ordinary drive-and-pitch variety, extra length off the tee offered little profit; placement for position seemed to be of paramount importance. Today, with the deadly pitching wedge used so proficiently by our better players, even on those holes of medium length, the long drive can be of advantage. It seems to me to be very definitely true that with steel shafts the players are able to hit more nearly all-out without too much risk of having the club betray them.

The net effect of all these things—improvement in balls, clubs and golf course maintenance—seems to me to have made the game easier. A better ball, better lies through the fairway, more regular and smoother putting surfaces, clubs better suited to their intended purposes and, perhaps above all, the more perfect balancing and matching of sets, all must contribute to the making of lower scores. . . .

JONES CLAIMED the U.S. Amateur trophy in 1927, three years before the Grand Slam, golf's "impregnable quadrilateral," consummated his reign.

> **Artifacts**

Slammer's Lid

Sam Snead's hat did more than protect Slammin' Sam's balding pate. It symbolized the man, his era and the tropical vacation the sun-chasing pro tour seemed to be. Snead's coconut straw hat also set a pattern for other golfers whose most distinctive gear was headgear

PAYNE STEWART
Sported retro knickers too

JESPER PARNEVIK
Put card company on his bill

SE RI PAK
Set style for "Seoul Sisters"

GREG NORMAN
Straw brims shaded Shark

MICHELLE McGANN
Easy to spot LPGA star

SHINGO KATAYAMA
Japan's self-branded "cowboy"

1997 | A PEBBLED beach wasn't the worst hazard for Fred Couples at the Masters—there was also Tiger Woods's 12-shot lead. | *Photograph by* JOHN BIEVER

1997 | NO FLOP with the wedge, Phil Mickelson won a Tour event as an amateur and 10 more as a pro by '97, but was still after his first major. | *Photograph by* ROBERT BECK

1959 | BLOND BOMBER Jack Nicklaus, 19, missed the U.S. Open cut but bounced back to take the trophy at the '59 U.S. Amateur. | *Photograph by* JOHN G. ZIMMERMAN

NANCY WITH THE LAUGHING FACE

BY FRANK DEFORD

A record-setting rookie's sudden success turned women's golf—
and her own life—upside down. —*from* SI, JULY 10, 1978

NANCY LOPEZ'S HOTEL ROOM is some kind of mess: clothes, clippings, cosmetics and candy Kisses, on account of this week happens to be Hershey, Pa. The p.r. man, exhausted from suddenly having to front for the eighth wonder of the world, flops on one bed. The guy from the country club, with pictures for Nancy to sign, stands in a clearing in the middle of the floor. The caddie is rounding up shoes and golf clubs and candy and today's swag. The first observation Nancy has about being famous is, "It's funny, but the more money I make, the more presents people give me."

The phone is ringing again. She picks her way through the forest of telegraphed roses and over some utter stranger who has found a seat on the floor. But what are you going to do? The day before, as she was getting dressed, three women reporters came in to watch and get a new angle. Luckily, today Nancy has just lost a tournament by 15 strokes; otherwise, she might be in some demand.

She talks on the phone standing up, there being no place to put anything down, herself included. She is a pack rat, but this is ridiculous. Growing up, the one rule was that she had to keep a neat room. Her father, Domingo, who has a third-grade education and an auto-body shop in Roswell, N.Mex., would not let her work. He would not even permit her to do the dishes. "No, Mama," he would tell Nancy's mother. "These hands are meant for golf." For five years she wore braces he could not afford. "Mama, she got to," Domingo said. "Our Nancy's gonna be a public figure." But at least she had to keep her room neat. Her father brought her up to be a champion, and her mother brought her up to be a lady; together they raised her as royalty, the countess of golf, *la condesa*, and she was just that in May of 1978 at age 21, and then she blows right by it in June to become the whole sport of women's golf. Even a countess can be expected to keep a neat room, but it is difficult for a person to manage that when her room contains a whole damn sport.

Nancy puts the phone down and sighs. "This is for the chairman," the guy with the pictures says. "Oh, he'll love this, Nancy."

"Think they'll want us back next year?" asks the p.r. man, Chip Campbell. All of a sudden Campbell is a bear with a gingersnap. . . .

Nancy turned pro last July and there were a number of second places before she finally won an LPGA tournament. Only a few months ago she would literally lie awake nights "wondering how I would react if ever I got the lead." She feared, mostly, that she would cave in, for she admits that too often then she played the prevailing LPGA style—trying to avoid bogeys rather than going for birdies. Considering how much golf affects her whole life, it is not surprising that she played it safe in other ways too. Succumbing to the loneliness that plagues so many traveling women athletes, she agreed to marry her college sweetheart, even though she well understood that this would divide her devotions and deny golf what she calls "mind time."

It was last Sept. 29 when Nancy's mother, Marina, died—with little warning—following an appendectomy. The grievous hurt was deepened, somehow made impossibly, unfairly worse by her certainty that Marina Lopez had been robbed of her life and her sacrifice too, just as the ship was to come in.

Nancy looks up, talking about this. It is odd, given her happy public aspect, but in fact her eyes are naturally mournful. Never was that more apparent. "I don't know what my mother's death did to me," she says, "except that somehow it made me more powerful mentally." And thus the question of how she would react when she got the lead was answered at last in February, in Sarasota, Fla., when she walked down the 72nd fairway, a stroke ahead, tears streaming down her face, thinking of her mother. She did not lose that lead.

That was the first, and the avalanche was about to begin: six more wins, including five in a row, and in that string the LPGA Championship in June. Total money winnings: $154,366—a record for a rookie, man or woman.

Along the way, Nancy called off her engagement. It had nothing to do with her fiancé, really. It was just, as she told him: "Now I know what I can do. . . ." She could win. She could go for the flag. So now Nancy is alone. . . .

AS A 21-year-old rookie out of the University of Tulsa, Lopez won five straight tournaments and became the leading light of women's golf.

HARRY BENSON

1995 | MONTEREY BAY sinks hookers and rewards onlookers on the 18th at
Pebble Beach, the most famous finishing hole on earth. | *Photograph by* JOHN BURGESS

1953 | PRESIDENT DWIGHT EISENHOWER got tips from his friend Arnold Palmer but still hit an Augusta National pine so often that it's now called the Eisenhower Tree. | *Photograph by* BETTMANN

> ## Golfers in Chief

Mister President, You're Away

Since Taft set the precedent, 15 of 18 chief executives have played the game. Their average handicap: 22

WILLIAM HOWARD TAFT

JOHN F. KENNEDY

RICHARD NIXON

GERALD FORD

RONALD REAGAN

GEORGE H.W. BUSH

BILL CLINTON

GEORGE W. BUSH

BARACK OBAMA

1995 | AFTER DUFFING a chip into the Valley of Sin, Costantino Rocca atoned with his putter to force a British Open playoff with John Daly. | *Photograph by* MIKE KING

from THE WAYS OF LIFE AT THE COUNTRY CLUB
BY ROBERT H. BOYLE | *SI, February 26, 1962*

IT SEEMS ODD NOW, BUT THE EARLY country clubs had no connection at all with golf. The first club formed was The Country Club in Brookline, Mass., in 1882. (It is a gaucherie of the worst sort to refer to the club as the Brookline Country Club. It is always The Country Club. As Dixon Wecter remarks in *The Saga of American Society*, The Country Club has never assumed a place name because "it is *sui generis*, like the roc's egg.")

The Country Club was the idea of James Murray Forbes, a proper Bostonian and a well-known sportsman and horseman. One of the coaching set, Forbes looked upon the Brookline countryside as the logical terminus for the then fashionable tally-ho drives. "The general idea," went the original prospectus, "is to have a comfortable clubhouse for the use of members and their families, a simple restaurant, bedrooms, bowling alley, lawn tennis grounds and so on; also to have race meetings and, occasionally, music in the afternoon." Horse racing was one of the main attractions at the club; there is still a track surrounding the first and 18th fairways. . . .

A great moment came in 1888 when John Reid, a Scot, banded together with five other congenial souls in Yonkers, N.Y., to build a golf course. They called their little group St. Andrews. The game caught on at established country clubs, whose members became enthusiastic about this latest sporting import from Britain. In Brookline, The Country Club, under prodding from such distinguished members as Arthur Hunnewell and G.E. Cabot, appropriated $50 for the construction of an experimental six-hole course. There is a legend that the spectators became quite bored watching the first match after one participant scored a hole in one on the 1st hole and the other players failed to duplicate the feat. In 1894 St. Andrews, The Country Club and three other clubs formed the U.S. Golf Association. The country club, energized by golf, was on its way. In Springfield, N.J., Louis Keller of *The Social Register* started Baltusrol, and up the Hudson River, Chauncey Depew and William Rockefeller helped to found the Ardsley Casino, forerunner of the present-day Ardsley Country Club.

The yellow press scoffed at these "howling swells" who golfed in scarlet jackets and leg wrappings, worn as protection against the nonexistent gorse, but to Henry James, returning to the U.S. in 1904 after a 30-year absence abroad, the country club was an object of admiration. It was the perfect place for the elite to relax. At the 19th hole of St. Andrews, Charles Schwab put together U.S. Steel by persuading Andrew Carnegie to sell out to J. P. Morgan. In Washington, William Howard Taft shrugged off Theodore Roosevelt's warning that golf was a dude's game. . . .

1889 | THIS IMAGE, the first golf photograph taken in America, shows the inaugural match played at St. Andrews Golf Club in Yonkers, N.Y. | *Photograph by* BROWN BROTHERS

2008 | TIED WITH Rocco Mediate on the 15th hole of a U.S. Open playoff,
Tiger Woods hung tough long enough to win on the 19th. | Photograph by FRED VUICH

1996 | LONG HITTER Laura Davies has won 20 LPGA titles and played in every Solheim Cup, helping lift Europe to three victories. | *Photograph by* BOB MARTIN

2005 | SWINGING OUT of her shoes for the Stars and Stripes, Solheim rookie Natalie Gulbis went 3–1 to help the U.S. claim the Cup. | *Photograph by* DARREN CARROLL

DAY OF GLORY FOR A GOLDEN OLDIE

BY RICK REILLY

At 46, Jack Nicklaus won his most dramatic Masters with a final-round 65 that had all of America cheering for him.
—*from* SI, APRIL 21, 1986

THAT ARM. WHO COULD FORGET that arm? In the roar of roars at the 18th green, from behind a Masters scoreboard glittering with the names of golf's power brokers—BALLESTEROS and WATSON and LANGER and KITE—under the sign that said No. 18, beside the huge black letters that read NICKLAUS, next to a red 9, came the arm that had put that number there, the arm that seconds before had placed a red 8 next to NORMAN, and that arm was pumping furiously.

No head, no body, no shoulder, just an arm belonging to the leader-board man, pumping and pumping for pure, wallowing joy. To hell with employee objectivity. Jack Nicklaus had just won the Masters, once again, and that arm just couldn't help itself. If it was Old St. Nick who had delivered the goodies; if it was the Ancient One who had posted that birdie at 17, then parred 18, while Greg Norman had taken out his Fore!-iron and mailed the gallery a souvenir on the same hole; if it was the Olden Bear who had mystically come from five shots and a couple of decades back to hijack the Masters golf tournament, then it was that arm behind the scoreboard that was telling us what it meant.

Can't you see? That red 9 set off an avalanche of history. Jack Nicklaus, a 46-year-old antique, had won his first green jacket in 11 years, his sixth over three decades and all in this, the 50th, and arguably the best, Masters.

How complete, how whole this was for Nicklaus. Hadn't he been duped out of that 20th long ago? Hadn't Tom Watson's chip taken the U.S. Open from him at Pebble Beach in 1982 and broken his spirit? How many times had he led a major only to have his pocket picked at the end? Now the spikes were on the other foot. Here was Nicklaus, in one swell swoop, reaching down from another era and snatching a major championship from the reigning czars of this one. It is a trick no other golf god has pulled, not Palmer or Hogan or Snead or Sarazen. Nicklaus had beaten young men at a young man's game on young men's greens and beaten them when they were at their youthful best. As Tom Kite, destiny's orphan, put it, "I hit nearly every shot the way I dreamed about today. But that's the strange thing about golf. You don't have any control about what your opponent does."

And just in the Nicklaus of time, too. Who else but Jack could save us from the woeful, doleful bowl full of American Express (do-you-know-me?) golf winners of late? And who else could play John Wayne, riding in to rescue the Yanks from golf's rampaging foreign legion: the dashingly handsome Seve Ballesteros of Spain; the stone-faced Bernhard Langer of West Germany; Australia's Norman, he of the colossal swing and larger-still reputation, more unfulfilled now than ever; and Zimbabwean-South African-Floridian Nick Price, who on Saturday broke the course record that had gone unsurpassed for 46 years, then on Sunday recoiled in the giant shadow of what he had done.

Here had come Nicklaus, an American legend still under warranty, armed with a putter the size of a Hoover attachment, denting the back of Augusta's holes with 25-foot putts at an age when most guys are afraid to take the putter back. Here had come Nicklaus, sending such a deluge of decibels into the Georgia air that lakes rippled and azaleas blushed; starting such a ruckus that grown men climbed trees, children rode on shoulders, concession-stand operators abandoned their posts, all just to tear off a swatch of history. Was that Jack in the checked pants and yellow shirt? Hmmmm. Yellow goes nice with green, doesn't it, Jack? You devil.

Maybe that was it. Maybe Nicklaus had drawn up a contract with Lucifer for one last major, for that slippery 20th that had eluded him since 1980, for a sixth green blazer. In exchange, Nicklaus would do pro-ams in Hades the rest of his days.

This is a guy who missed the cut at the Honda, for the love of Hogan. In fact, Nicklaus missed the cut in three of seven tournaments this year and withdrew from a fourth. Of the ones he finished, his most impressive showing was a tie for 39th at the Hawaiian Open, which didn't exactly throw a scare into Corey Pavin, who won. The $144,000 for winning the Masters means he's up to $148,404 for the year. . . .

"I finally found that guy I used to know on the golf course," Nicklaus told his wife, Barbara. "It was me." . . .

WITH SON JACKIE serving as his caddie, the Golden Bear shot 30 on the final nine to claim his sixth Masters.

1997 | A GATHERING STORM couldn't scatter fans behind the 18th green, though it would halt the International for two hours. | *Photograph by* JOE MAHONEY

1959 | A GOLF BOOM saw Arnie's Army attracting recruits like this pair piloting a three-wheeled cart in Palm Springs. | *Photograph by* JOHN G. ZIMMERMAN

> **Artifacts**

Soles Worth Saving

A century of evolution has brought shoes that are gentler on greens, quieter on cart paths and louder to look at.

FRANCIS OUIMET | The 1913 U.S. Open hero kicked off American golf's golden age.

BOBBY LOCKE | The mid-century putting genius wore white while stalking greens.

BERNHARD LANGER | The Euros' captain sported soft spikes at the 2004 Ryder Cup.

BEN HOGAN | Bantam Ben had his Fifties-era models
custom-made with extra spikes for stability.

JOHNNY MILLER | Miller laced up this patriotic
pair, then shot 63 to win the 1973 U.S. Open.

DAVID N. BERKWITZ: THIS PAGE AND OPPOSITE. TOP: USGA MUSEUM. OPPOSITE PAGE, BOTTOM ROW: WORLD GOLF HALL OF FAME.

1920s | AT THE APEX of his game, photography pioneer George Lewis took aim atop the Pyramid of Cheops in Giza, Egypt. | *Photograph by* USGA MUSEUM

1990 | FOUR STEPS to success: Open stance and club face, strike the sand behind the ball, follow through, make the putt. | *Photograph by* LEONARD KAMSLER

THE BOGEY MAN

BY GEORGE PLIMPTON

A hacker with a history of throwing himself to the lions tried playing with the touring pros and detailed the experience for SI. What follows is the first in a three-part series that became a classic book.
—*from* SI, JANUARY 30, 1967

I HAD A NOTION THAT A MONTH ON the professional golf tour, competing steadily and under tournament conditions before crowds and under the scrutiny of the pros with whom I would be playing, might result in five, perhaps even six, strokes being pruned from my handicap, which is 18. My friends thought so too. They envied me my invitations to the Bing Crosby National Pro-Amateur, the Lucky International in San Francisco and the Bob Hope Desert Classic in Palm Springs—the near month of tournament play in the pro-ams that I would enjoy on the tour—and they said that the one compensation they could think of as they toiled at their desks was that on my return I would not be as likely to embarrass them with my bad golf on our occasional weekend rounds.

I was hopeful but also uneasy, aware that quite an overhaul of my game was going to be necessary. My woes in golf, I have felt, have been largely psychological. When I am playing well, in the low 90s, I am still plagued with small quirks—a suspicion that, for example, just as I begin my downswing, my eyes straining with concentration, a bug or a beetle is suddenly going to materialize on the ball. And when I am playing badly far more massive speculation occurs: I often sense as I commit myself to a golf swing that my body changes its corporeal status completely and becomes a *mechanical* entity, built of tubes and conduits and boiler rooms here and there, with big dials and gauges to check, a Brobdingnagian structure put together by a team of brilliant engineers but manned by a dispirited, eccentric group of dissolutes.

I see myself as a monstrous, manned colossus poised high over the golf ball, a spheroid that is barely discernible 14 stories down on its tee. From above, staring through the windows of the eyes, which bulge like great bay porches, is an unsteady group (as I see them) of retired Japanese navy men. In their hands they hold ancient and useless voice tubes into which they yell the familiar orders: "Eye on the ball! Chin steady! Left arm stiff! Flex the knees! Swing from the inside out! Follow through! Keep head down!" Since the voice tubes are useless, the cries drift down the long corridors and shaftways between the iron tendons and muscles and echo into vacant chambers and out, until finally, as a burble of sound, they reach the control centers. These posts are situated at the joints, and in charge are the dissolutes I mentioned—typical of them a cantankerous elder perched on a metal stool, half a bottle of rye on the floor beside him, his ear cocked for the orders that he acknowledges with ancient epithets, yelling back up the corridors, "Ah, your father's mustache" and such things, and if he's of a mind he'll reach for the controls (like the banks of tall levers one remembers from a railroad-yard switch house) and perhaps he'll pull the proper lever and perhaps not. So that, in sum, the whole apparatus, bent on hitting a golf ball smartly, tips and convolutes and lunges, the Japanese navy men clutching each other for support in the main control center up in the head as the structure rocks and creaks. And when the golf shot is on its way the observers get to their feet and peer out through the eyes and report: "A shank! A shank! My God, we've hit another shank!"

The Japanese navy men stir about and shout, "Smarten up down there!"

In the dark reaches of the structure the dissolutes reach for their rye, tittering, and they've got their feet up on the levers and perhaps soon it will be time to read the evening newspaper.

When I got out to the Monterey Peninsula, where the Crosby is played, and met some of the professional golfers, I asked them timidly if such wayward thoughts ever popped into their minds at a moment of crisis on the course—some image quite apart from golf.

Well, what sort of thoughts, they wanted to know.

I told them, somewhat haltingly, about the retired Japanese naval officers, a phenomenon I had never been able to explain to myself, and they stared and said, well no, they weren't harassed by any such thoughts as *that*. If pressed, they would admit to an inner voice, cajoling and murmuring encouragement. Dave Marr told me that, as he stood over his putt on the 16th green during the PGA Championship he won at Laurel Valley in 1965, clear as a bell he heard his baby's voice call in his head, "Careful, Daddy, careful!"—just as the baby did when he was being tossed joyfully in the air, roughhousing at home. Marr, hearing his son's voice, *was* careful, so careful that his putt ended up short. He two-putted from there. . . .

WHILE PLIMPTON'S body English stammered, his crusty caddie offered a remedy: "Why don't you go and get yourself some good advice?"

RUSS HALFORD

1951 | WITHOUT A LAPTOP in sight, reporters covered a Masters duel between Ben Hogan and Skee Riegel that ended predictably. | *Photograph by* MILLER BROWN

1993 | THE CADDIES of Pinehurst took a break to add "pony up" to the old looper mantra, "Show up, shut up and keep up." | *Photograph by* BILL FRAKES

1979 | JACK'S PACK, also known as the Golden Bear's gallery, framed its favorite at Augusta National. | *Photograph by* HEINZ KLUETMEIER

2001 | DRIVING HOMEWARD at the Masters, Tiger Woods made Augusta's 18th his corridor of power. | *Photograph by* FRED VUICH

1931 – 1954

The Dawn *of the* Tour

JIMMY DEMARET
At the PGA Championship
1936
Photograph by BETTMANN

THE ERA'S BEST

Ben Hogan

He overcame his father's suicide, a chronic hook, a stint in the Army Air Corps during his prime and a near-fatal car accident in 1949 to win nine majors and golf immortality.

Sam Snead

Slammin' Sam triumphed in more than 140 events worldwide, with a record 82 tour titles including seven majors, and may have been the best pure athlete ever to play the game.

Byron Nelson

The courtly Lord Byron, who helped develop the modern golf swing, will always be remembered for the way he reigned during 1945, when he won 18 tournaments including 11 in a row.

Babe Didrikson Zaharias

The most versatile female athlete of all time captured 10 majors after taking up golf on a day off during the 1932 Olympics, in which she won two gold medals in track and field.

Jimmy Demaret

A fashion plate and bon vivant, Demaret was also a fierce competitor who collected three Masters titles. In 1940 he won five straight tournaments on his way to the green jacket.

>MILESTONES<

1931
BILLY CASPER
Born June 24

1934
FIRST MASTERS >
Horton Smith wins

1935
GARY PLAYER
Born November 1

1937
HARRY VARDON
Dies at age 66

1939
RYDER CUP
Canceled due to World War II

1940
JACK NICKLAUS
Born January 21

1946
BYRON NELSON
Retires at age 34

1949
BEN HOGAN
Nearly killed in car crash

1949
TOM WATSON
Born September 4

1950
LPGA
Tampa Open is first-ever event

NOW OPEN FOR PLAY

Augusta National
AUGUSTA, GEORGIA
1933 / Designed by Alister MacKenzie & Bobby Jones
< THE POND ADDED TO AUGUSTA'S 16TH IN THE
1950s MADE THE HOLE A TOUGHER TEST.

Shinnecock Hills
SOUTHAMPTON, NEW YORK
1931 / William Flynn

Royal Melbourne
MELBOURNE, AUSTRALIA
1932 / Alister MacKenzie & Alex Russell

Southern Hills
TULSA, OKLAHOMA
1936 / Perry Maxwell

>> GOLF IN THE REAL WORLD <<

Bing's Fling May 22, 1950 Crooner Bing Crosby, who had launched his eponymous Pro-Am in 1937, enters the British Amateur at St. Andrews, only to lose in the first round to local contractor Jim Wilson. Throngs of screaming Scottish bobbysoxers follow the match.

Heavy Hitter January 17, 1952 Former heavyweight champ Joe Louis enters the San Diego Open as an amateur. Louis's quest becomes a cause célèbre after he is initially rejected because he is black. Columnist and radio star Walter Winchell rallies nationwide support for Louis, who tees it up. The first African-American to play in a PGA-sanctioned event misses the cut by eight strokes; black pros remain banned from the tour for almost a decade.

Pay to Play August 9, 1953 The Tam O'Shanter World Championship becomes the first nationally televised golf tournament—by paying ABC to carry it. Lew Worsham holes out a wedge for eagle to win.

Who's Dino's Caddy? August 10, 1953 Jerry Lewis plays a loopy looper to a PGA pro portrayed by Dean Martin in the comedy classic *The Caddy*. In the film, their high jinks catch the eye of a talent agent who convinces Martin and Lewis to form a comedy team.

Jimmy Loves Lucy May 17, 1954 In an effort to keep their wives ⅂ from taking up golf, Ricky and Fred concoct impossible rules. The plan backfires when three-time Masters champion Jimmy Demaret teams up with Lucy and Ethel to show the men who's boss.

Houston, We Have a Solution June 2, 1954 Two weeks after the U.S. Supreme Court prohibits school segregation in *Brown v. Board of Education*, the city of Houston lifts its long-standing whites-only policy at municipal courses in reaction to *Beal v. Holcombe*, a case filed by five African-American golfers.

A wife asks, "Why don't you play golf with Tom O'Brien?" Her husband says, "Would you play with a foul-mouthed, drunken, lying cheat? No? Well, neither will Tom O'Brien."

BEST SHOT

APRIL 7, 1935

Gene Sarazen

Standing 235 yards from the flag on the 15th at Augusta, Sarazen laces his second shot, a four-wood, that reaches the green and falls into the hole for a double-eagle deuce. Reporters dub it "The Shot Heard 'round the World."

WORST SHOT

JUNE 15, 1947

Sam Snead

The Slammer misses a 30-inch putt to lose an 18-hole playoff to Lew Worsham in the U.S. Open at St. Louis Country Club—one of Snead's four second-place finishes at the Open, the only major that will elude him.

> THE SWING   *A strong, limber athlete, SAM SNEAD focused on keeping his head steady and his chest over the ball at impact.*

> GOLF EVOLVES

A NEW WEAPON After concave-faced "spoon" clubs are banned in 1931, Gene Sarazen designs a flat-faced wedge that slides through sand, lifting sand and ball from a bunker. Once Sarazen wins the '32 U.S and British Opens, everyone wants a sand wedge.

STABLEFORD SCORING Designed by scratch golfer Dr. Frank Stableford in 1931, the "modern" system awards three points for each birdie and one for each bogey.

STYMIES BLOCKED An age-old tactic called the stymie bites the dust: Before 1950, a player had to knock his ball over or around another ball blocking his path to the cup. Now his opponent must mark the offending ball. The USGA outlaws the stymie in '50 and the R&A follows suit the next year.

STROKE AND DISTANCE The two-shot penalty for balls hit out-of-bounds becomes the worldwide standard after an epic USGA/R&A rules conference in 1951.

GAME CHANGER: THE GOLF CART
Developed after World War II to make the game more accessible to handicapped veterans and senior citizens, motorized carts also speed the pace of play—when used right—though purists still insist on walking.

> ON THE NUMBER

13 Founding members of the LPGA, which teed off in 1950 with Patty Berg, Marlene Hagge, Betty Jameson, Louise Suggs, Babe Didrikson Zaharias and eight others playing 14 tournaments with an average purse of $3,500.

59 Days Ben Hogan spent in an El Paso hospital after a near-fatal head-on collision between his Cadillac and a Greyhound bus on February 2, 1949.

14 Clubs allowed in the bag by a 1938 USGA ruling. Players had often used up to 25 sticks; '36 U.S. Open champ Tony Manero carried 19.

2 Purple Hearts awarded to Lloyd Mangrum for his heroics during World War II. Army staff sergeant Mangrum suffered a broken arm at the Battle of Normandy and multiple shrapnel wounds during the Battle of the Bulge, then won the first postwar U.S. Open in 1946.

13 Second-place finishes for Harold "Jug" McSpaden in 1945, the year his friend and match-play partner Byron Nelson had 18 victories, including 11 in a row.

72 Extra holes it took Billy Burke to defeat George Von Elm at Inverness in 1931 during the longest U.S. Open playoff ever.

>> FROM THE VAULT

"BEN TREASURED HIS PRIVACY, *and I respected that. He was a peculiar person, and I'm a peculiar person, so it's no surprise that ours was a peculiar relationship. I was never in Ben's home, and I didn't have his private telephone number. Yet I think I was probably Ben's best friend on the pro tour....*"

—BYRON NELSON EULOGIZING BEN HOGAN *in* SI, AUGUST 4, 1997

1948 | TIRELESS BEN HOGAN "dug it out of the dirt" on the practice range and out of the carpet while wife Valerie looked on. | *Photograph by* LOOMIS DEAN

1962 | SWINGIN' SIXTIES TV producer Sy Gomberg risked his wife to beat balls at a plastic sheet in their living room. | *Photograph by* RUSS HALFORD

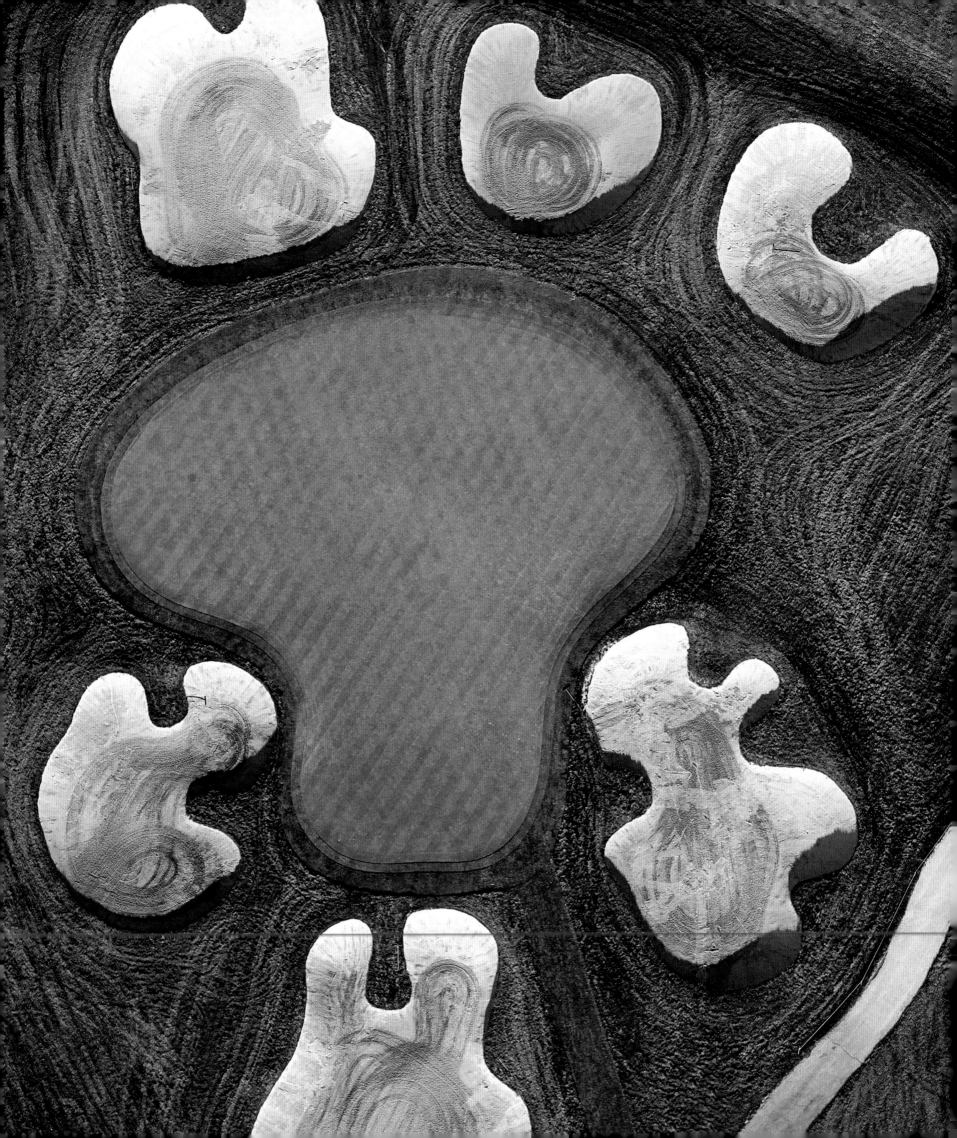

1994 | SAY YOUR PRAYERS before visiting the Church Pews at Oakmont Country Club, hellish for all but Ernie Els at the '94 U.S. Open. | *Photograph by* FRED VUICH

2007 | DUFFERS FEAR the Dubsdread Course at Cog Hill Country Club in Lemont, Ill., site of Tiger Woods's 60th PGA Tour victory. | *Photograph by* VINCENT LAFORET

1997 | ONE TWOSOME putted at Virginia's Meadows Farm Golf Course while another putt-putted toward the 841-yard par-6 hole ahead. | *Photograph by* WALTER P. CALAHAN

1996 | COLIN MONTGOMERIE disappointed Monty-haters who hoped the dour Scot would restrict his long walks to short piers. | *Photograph by* DAVID CANNON

THE CHOSEN ONE

BY GARY SMITH

Tiger Woods was raised to believe that his destiny was to be the best golfer ever, and to change the world. Would the pressures of fame grind him down first? —*from* SI, DECEMBER 23, 1996

IT WAS ORDINARY. IT WAS OH SO ordinary. It was a salad, a dinner roll, a steak, a half potato, a slice of cake, a clinking fork, a podium joke, a ballroom full of white-linen-tablecloth conversation. Then a thick man with tufts of white hair rose from the head table. His voice trembled and his eyes teared and his throat gulped down sobs between words, and everything ordinary was cast out of the room.

He said, "Please forgive me...but sometimes I get very emotional...when I talk about my son.... My heart...fills with *so*... *much*...*joy*...when I realize...that this young man...is going to be able...to help so many people.... He will transcend this game...and bring to the world...a humanitarianism...which has never been known before. The world will be a better place to live in...by virtue of his existence...and his presence....I acknowledge only a small part in that...in that I know that I was personally selected by God himself...to nurture this young man...and bring him to the point where he can make his contribution to humanity.... This is my treasure.... Please accept it...and use it wisely....Thank you."

Blinking tears, the man found himself inside the arms of his son and the applause of the people, all up on their feet.

IN THE history of American celebrity, no father has ever spoken this way. Too many dads have deserted or died before their offspring reached this realm, but mostly they have fallen mute, the father's vision exceeded by the child's, leaving the child to wander, lost, through the sad and silly wilderness of modern fame.

So let us stand amidst this audience at last month's Fred Haskins Award dinner to honor America's outstanding college golfer of 1996, and take note as Tiger and Earl Woods embrace, for a new manner of celebrity is taking form before our eyes. Regard the 64-year-old African-American father, arm upon the superstar's shoulder, right where the chip is so often found, declaring that this boy will do more good for the world than any man who ever walked it. Gaze at the 20-year-old son, with the blood of four races in his veins, not flinching an inch from the yoke of his father's prophecy but already beginning to scent the complications. The son who stormed from behind to win a record third straight U.S. Amateur last August, turned pro and rang up scores in the 60s in 21 of his first 27 rounds, winning two PGA Tour events as he doubled and tripled the usual crowds and dramatically changed their look and age.

Now turn. Turn and look at us, the audience, standing in anticipation of something different, something pure. *Quiet.* Just below the applause, or within it, can you hear the grinding? That's the relentless chewing mechanism of fame, girding to grind the purity and the promise to dust. Not the promise of talent, but the bigger promise, the father's promise, the one that stakes everything on the boy's not becoming separated from his own humanity and from all the humanity crowding around him.

It's a fitting moment, while he's up there at the head table with the audience on its feet, to anoint Eldrick (Tiger) Woods— the rare athlete to establish himself *immediately* as the dominant figure in his sport—as SPORTS ILLUSTRATED's 1996 Sportsman of the Year. And to pose a question: Who will win? The machine...or the youth who has just entered its maw?

TIGER WOODS will win. He'll fulfill his father's vision because of his mind, one that grows more still, more willful, more efficient, the greater the pressure upon him grows.

The machine will win because it has no mind. It flattens even as it lifts, trivializes even as it exalts, spreads a man so wide and thin that he becomes margarine soon enough.

Tiger will win because of God's mind. *Can't you see the pattern?* Earl Woods asks. *Can't you see the signs?* "Tiger will do more than any other man in history to change the course of humanity," Earl says.

Sports history, Mr. Woods? Do you mean more than Joe Louis and Jackie Robinson, more than Muhammad Ali and Arthur Ashe? "More than any of them because he's more charismatic, more educated, more prepared for this than anyone."

Anyone, Mr. Woods? Your son will have more impact than Nelson Mandela, more than Gandhi, more than Buddha?

"Yes, because he has a larger forum than any of them. Because he's playing a sport that's international. Because he's qualified through his ethnicity to accomplish miracles. He's the bridge between the East and the West. There is no limit

TOUR ROOKIE Woods, three weeks shy of his 21st birthday, had already won two pro events and a Sportsman of the Year award.

because he has the guidance. I don't know yet exactly what form this will take. But he is the Chosen One. He'll have the power to impact nations. Not people. *Nations.* The world is just getting a taste of his power."

Surely this is lunacy. Or are we just too myopic to see? One thing is certain: We are witnessing the first volley of an epic encounter, the machine at its mightiest confronting the individual groomed all his life to conquer it and turn it to his use. The youth who has been exposed to its power since he toddled onto *The Mike Douglas Show* at three, the set of *That's Incredible!* at five, the boy who has been steeled against the silky seduction to which so many before him have succumbed. The one who, by all appearances, brings more psychological balance, more sense of self, more consciousness of possibility to the battlefield than any of his predecessors.

This is war, so let's start with war. Remove the images of pretty putting greens from the movie screen standing near the ballroom's head table. Jungle is what's needed here, foliage up to a man's armpits, sweat trickling down his thighs, leeches crawling up them. Lieut. Col. Earl Woods, moving through the night with his rifle ready, wondering why a U.S. Army public information officer stationed in Brooklyn decided in his mid-30s that he belonged in the Green Berets and ended up doing two tours of duty in Vietnam. Wondering why his first marriage has died and why the three children from it have ended up without a dad around when it's dark like this and it's time for bed—just as Earl ended up as a boy after his own father died. Wondering why he keeps plotting ways to return to the line of fire—"creative soldiering," he calls it—to eyeball death once more. To learn once again about his dark and cold side, the side that enables Earl, as Tiger will remark years later, "to slit your throat and then sit down and eat his dinner."

Oh, yes, Earl is one hell of a cocktail. A little Chinese, a little Cherokee, a few shots of African-American; don't get finicky about measurements, we're making a vat here. Pour in some gruffness and a little intimidation, then some tenderness

and some warmth and a few jiggers of old anger. Don't hold back on intelligence. And stoicism. Add lots of stoicism, and even more of responsibility—"the most responsible son of a bitch you've ever seen in your life" is how Earl himself puts it. Top it all with "a bucket of whiskey," which is what he has been known to order when he saunters into a bar and he's in the mood. Add a dash of hyperbole, maybe two, and to hell with the ice, just whir. This is one of those concoctions you're going to remember when morning comes.

Somewhere in there, until a good 15 years ago, there was one other ingredient, the existential Tabasco, the smoldering why? The Thai secretary in the U.S. Army office in Bangkok smelled it soon after she met Earl, in 1967. "He couldn't relax," says Kultida (Tida) Woods. "Searching for something, always searching, never satisfied. I think because both his parents died when he was young, and he didn't have mom and dad to make him warm. Sometimes he stayed awake till three or four in the morning, just thinking."

In a man so accustomed to exuding command and control, in a Green Beret lieutenant colonel, *why?* has a way of building up power like a river dammed. Why did the Vietcong sniper bracket him that day (first bullet a few inches left of one ear, second bullet a few inches right of the other) but never fire the third bullet? Why did Earl's South Vietnamese combat buddy, Nguyen Phong—the one Earl nicknamed Tiger, and in whose memory he would nickname his son—stir one night just in time to awaken Earl and warn him not to budge because a viper was poised inches from his right eye? What about that road Earl's jeep rolled down one night, the same road on which two friends had just been mutilated, the road that took him through a village so silent and dark that his scalp tingled, and then, just beyond it . . . hell turned inside-out over his shoulder, the sky lighting up and all the huts he had just passed spewing Vietcong machine-gun and artillery fire? He never understands what is the purpose of Lieutenant Colonel Woods's surviving again and again. He never quite comprehends what is the point of his life, until. . . .

THE PACKAGING of the phenom began at Nike headquarters, where marketing executives prepped Woods for life as a multimedia star.

Until the boy is born. He will get all the time that Earl was unable to devote to the three children from his first marriage. He will be the only child from Earl's second marriage, to the Thai woman he brought back to America, and right away there are signs. What other six-month-old, Earl asks, has the balance to stand in the palm of his father's hand and remain there even as Daddy strolls around the house? Was there another 11-month-old, ever, who could pick up a sawed-off club, imitate his father's golf swing so fluidly and drive the ball so wickedly into the nylon net across the garage? Another four-year-old who could be dropped off at the golf course at 9 a.m. on a Saturday and picked up at 5 p.m., pockets bulging with money he had won from disbelievers 10 and 20 years older, until Pop said, "Tiger, you can't do that"? Earl starts to get a glimmer. He is to be the father of the world's most gifted golfer.

But *why*? What for? Not long after Tiger's birth, when Earl has left the military to become a purchaser for McDonnell Douglas, he finds himself in a long discussion with a woman he knows. She senses the power pooling inside him, the friction. "You have so much to give," she tells him, "but you're not giving it. You haven't even scratched the surface of your potential." She suggests he try est, Erhard Seminars Training, an intensive self-discovery and self-actualizing technique, and it hits Earl hard, direct mortar fire to the heart. What he learns is that his overmuscular sense of responsibility for others has choked his potential.

"To the point," says Earl, "that I wouldn't even buy a handkerchief for myself. It went all the way back to the day my father died, when I was 11, and my mother put her arm around me after the funeral and said, 'You're the man of the house now.' I became the father that young, looking out for everyone else, and then she died two years later.

"What I learned through est was that by doing more for myself, I could do much more for others. Yes, be responsible, but *love* life, and give people the space to be in your life, and allow yourself room to give to others. That caring and sharing is what's most important, not being responsible for everyone else. Which is where Tiger comes in. What I learned led me to give so much time to Tiger, and to give him the space to be himself, and not to smother him with dos and don'ts. I took out the authority aspect and turned it into companionship. I made myself vulnerable as a parent. When you have to earn respect from your child, rather than demanding it because it's owed to you as the father, miracles happen. I realized that, through him, the giving could take a quantum leap. What I could do on a limited scale, he could do on a global scale."

At last, the river is undammed, and Earl's whole life makes sense. At last, he sees what he was searching for, a pattern. No more volunteering for missions—he has his. Not simply to be a great golfer's father. To be destiny's father. His son will change the world. . . .

Maybe it has to do with timing: the appearance of his son when America is turning the corner to a century in which the country's faces of color will nearly equal those that are white. Maybe, every now and then, a man gets swallowed by the machine, but the machine is changed more than he is.

For when we swallow Tiger Woods, the yellow-black-red-white man, we swallow something much more significant than Michael Jordan or Charles Barkley. We swallow hope in the American experiment, in the pell-mell jumbling of genes. We swallow the belief that the face of the future is not necessarily a bitter or bewildered face; that it might even, one day, be something like Tiger Woods's face: handsome and smiling and ready to kick all comers' asses.

We see a woman, 50-ish and Caucasian, well-coiffed and tailored—the woman we see at every country club—walk up to Tiger Woods before he receives the Haskins Award and say, "When I watch you taking on all those other players, Tiger, I feel like I'm watching my own son". . . and we feel the quivering of the cosmic compass that occurs when human beings look into the eyes of someone of another color and see their own flesh and blood.

> TIGER WOODS WILL WIN. HE'LL FULFILL HIS FATHER'S VISION BECAUSE OF HIS MIND, ONE THAT GROWS MORE STILL, MORE WILLFUL, MORE EFFICIENT, THE GREATER THE PRESSURE UPON HIM GROWS.

> **Artifacts**

Peg of High Art

Morphing from a mound of sand to the latest low-friction wonder, the humble tee keeps elevating its game

1930s
Silver tee clip

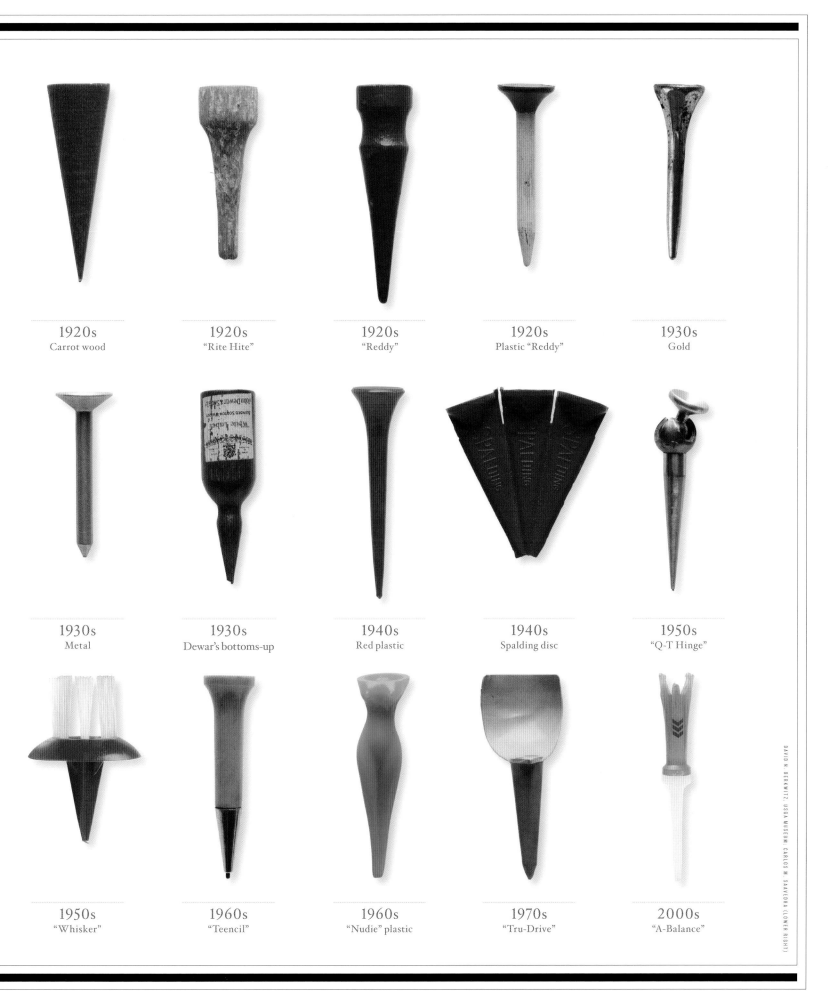

| 1920s | 1920s | 1920s | 1920s | 1930s |
| Carrot wood | "Rite Hite" | "Reddy" | Plastic "Reddy" | Gold |

| 1930s | 1930s | 1940s | 1940s | 1950s |
| Metal | Dewar's bottoms-up | Red plastic | Spalding disc | "Q-T Hinge" |

| 1950s | 1960s | 1960s | 1970s | 2000s |
| "Whisker" | "Teencil" | "Nudie" plastic | "Tru-Drive" | "A-Balance" |

1923 | THE SHORT GAME preoccupied sand-wedge inventor Gene Sarazen (left) and comic Buster Keaton, who introduced the Squire to minigolf. | *Photograph by* USGA MUSEUM

1934 | SWING SCIENTISTS Al Watrous, Bobby Jones, Tommy Armour and Billy Burke (left to right) checked an early golfbot's mechanics. | *Photograph by* BETTMANN

MASTER STROKES

BY RICK REILLY

April of '96 proved to be the cruelest month for golf's Great White Shark, harpooned by fate and Nick Faldo.

—*from* SI, APRIL 22, 1996

O N THE DRIVE TO THE GOLF course she saw a graveyard, and she secretly held her breath, closed her eyes and made a wish. When your dad is Greg Norman you stop trusting Sundays and you start working all the angles you can, six-shot lead or no six-shot lead. But by the end of the day Morgan-Leigh Norman, 13, was just another mourner in a green-carpeted funeral procession, a red-eyed witness to the blackest golfing day of her father's life, the day he somehow spent all six of those shots and five more besides, stilled 50,000 people and turned a glorious spring afternoon at the Masters into a 4½-hour cringe. "I been to several state fairs," an old Augusta native said, trudging home in the dying light, "and I ain't never seen nothin' like that."

It happened so quickly, it was hard to say what had been seen. A swing buried in a bunker at the start, three straight bogeys in the middle, a Maxfli in the water at the 12th and another at the 16th. Suddenly Norman's greatest rival, Nick Faldo, was walking past him straight into the green jacket that had been fashioned all week for Norman.

The last 20 minutes were unlike any seen in the previous 59 Masters. Norman became a kind of dead man walking, four shots behind and all his dreams drowning in Augusta National ponds behind him. Spectators actually looked down, hoping not to make eye contact, as Norman passed among them on his way to the 18th tee. At the finish, as Faldo made a meaningless 15-foot birdie putt, the champion was unsure how to handle it. He barely raised his hands above his head, and he didn't yell or dance. He looked like a man in the back of church who had won a clandestine hand of gin. After he finally took the accomplice ball out of the cup, he turned to Norman, hugged him long and hard and said, "I don't know what to say. I just want to give you a hug. I feel horrible about what happened. I'm so sorry." Both men teared up.

Even for Norman, who has a master's in how to lose these things—from ahead to Tom Watson in '81, from behind to Jack Nicklaus in '86, from nowhere to Larry Mize in '87, from everywhere to Ben Crenshaw in '95—this was gruesome. So the morning papers were right after all. They had predicted a runaway, and they had gotten it. Only the idea had been to hold an 18-hole parade in Norman's honor to make up for all the broken hearts and second-place crystal he had lugged home over the years. It would be his payback for having had to wait longer than any champion for his green jacket (16 years).

The green-jacket ceremony, however, was conducted as though Norman had been taken away by ambulance. "Our sincerest feelings go out to Greg," said Crenshaw, the presenter. "I do feel sorry for Greg," said Faldo, the recipient.

If you had been there the night before, you would not have believed what would transpire in less than 24 hours. In Saturday's third round Norman had stared down Faldo heroically, played him head-to-head and increased his lead from four to six shots. Afterward Norman relaxed in the dark of Augusta's first-floor locker room, the one reserved for nonchampions. He had been the last one off the course, and the attendant had turned out the lights and gone home. Norman didn't know how to turn them back on, so he just sat there in the dark, happily drained. "Your last night in this locker room," a friend had told him.

"Damn, I hope so," Norman had replied, laughing.

Then something eerie happened. A well-meaning British friend accosted Norman, held him by both shoulders, grinned wildly and said, "Greg, old boy, there's no way you can f--- this up now!" Norman thanked him with a castor-oil smile and walked out into the Georgia night alone.

This *had* seemed like a happy ending that even Norman couldn't rewrite. Luck was supposed to have left him long ago and taken the car and the dog with it, but this week luck had been back with him, nuzzling his face. For instance, on Wednesday his back was hurting so badly that he left the course two hours early, unable to make much more than a half swing. "He was just so *frustrated*," said his wife, Laura. "It hadn't happened to him in forever. He kept saying, 'Why now, of all times?'"

So who calls up out of the blue? Fred Couples. He had heard the Shark was ailing, and he offered to send over his back therapist, Tom Boers, to fix him up. Boers is the miracle-thumbed genius who had fixed Couples up two weeks earlier, allowing him to win the Players Championship. He fixed Norman up too. On Thursday the Shark opened with a course-record-tying 63. . . .

THE STRICKEN, star-crossed Norman floundered in the final round after leading the Masters by half a dozen shots.

1974 | A BIGGER hit off the course than on it, Laura Baugh had 10 runner-up finishes but no victories in 25 LPGA seasons. | *Photograph by* LEONARD KAMSLER

1964 | AFTER LEARNING to play with a guava-tree branch, Puerto Rico's Chi Chi Rodriguez had a blast swinging persimmon drivers. | *Photograph by* RUSS HALFORD

2001 | THAT SINKING feeling elated Jim Furyk, who sank a bunker shot to stay alive in his NEC playoff with Tiger Woods. | *Photograph by* FRED VUICH

1974 | LEE ELDER vaulted to victory at the Monsanto Open, earning the right to break the Masters' color line the following spring. | *Photograph by* BETTMANN

FUN TIMES
IN THE THIRTIES

BY DAN JENKINS

The pros drove sedans and Spalding Dots, played for peanuts and blazed a trail for future millionaires. —from SI, APRIL 4, 1966

BOY, *THOSE* THIRTIES. FUN TIME. The years when Sam Snead had hair, right there on his head, parted on the left; when Ben Hogan was a runt with a wild hook and a snap-brim hat; when Jimmy Demaret had pink shoes and violet pants; when Ky Laffoon anointed the greens with tobacco juice; and when Ruby Keeler and Dick Powell, in their sailor suits, couldn't do the Big Apple much better than Joan and Paul Runyan or Emma and Harry Cooper. It was Fun Time, all right, Fun Time on the pro golf tour—because if you couldn't laugh about it you might as well go back to mowing fairways and raking cottonseed-hull greens.

The game still belonged to the amateurs in the early thirties, you see, to aristocratic young men with hyphenated names and blonde sisters. A professional was anyone who had caddied after he was 14, who could wrap leather grips and who took his meals in the kitchen. The exact date is not recorded when people first realized a pro could make a nine-iron back up better than an amateur, but it happened somewhere in the thirties. At about the same time Walter Hagen finally convinced everyone you could let a pro in the front door and he wouldn't steal the crystal. These two circumstances began to combine, introducing America to the age of the alligator shoe. This, then, was the beginning of the era that launched the big-money tour.

If you shot over 74 in the first round you could forget it—15th was the last pay spot and, of the 30 to 40 regulars who were beating you, Ben Hogan was about the least known. But leaving town was always the same. You loaded into somebody's Graham-Paige or Essex and drove until you threw a connecting rod. Air travel? That was for Noah Beery Jr. up there in the sleet without any deicers while Jean Rogers wept softly in the radio tower.

The tour began in Los Angeles, just as it does now, but there the similarity ends. Everyone piled into the Hollywood Plaza for $1 a day, went directly downstairs to Clara Bow's It Cafe and began contemplating the happy fact that L.A. offered one of the biggest purses on the tour. And, next to the U.S. Open, it pulled the most spectators—so many one year, in fact, that in the congested excitement of a certain round Dick Metz had to park two miles away from the course and buy a ticket to get in. This would not have been so embarrassing for the sponsors if Metz hadn't been leading the tournament at the time.

From L.A. you went to Agua Caliente or Sacramento, maybe, or you scooped wedges around the Rose Bowl in the Pasadena Open. Wherever you were, you stuffed the bag with oranges from the citrus trees in the rough. It kept the food budget down. At the San Francisco Match Play you spewed challenges at anyone in the locker room you figured you could beat, and tried to get the pairings arranged accordingly.

In Florida the pros got their first inkling that they might be some kind of semicelebrities. It was all because of the Miami-Biltmore Four-Ball, a partnership tournament sponsored by a hotel that figured sports-page stories with the word Biltmore in them might give rewarding ideas to tourists. The Miami-Biltmore also may have invented appearance money, for it always paid the Open and PGA champions $1,000 each to show up, as if they had anywhere else to go. The whole field got a bottle of White Horse Scotch and a tin of Lucky Strikes for each birdie. And every day both players and wives were hoisted by autogyros over to Miami Beach for a swim. If at any time the sponsors grew lax at providing entertainment, the players took over. Such as the evening that Walter Hagen came back from a fishing trip and dumped his entire catch, including an alligator, into the clubhouse.

The old tour was no sooner meeting Snead than along came a quite different newcomer, Ben Hogan. He was a loner and a brooder with an uncontrollable hook who had about everyone convinced that he would never make it. Devoting every waking hour to his game, Hogan warmed up to only a few of his contemporaries—mainly to Demaret, his four-ball partner, to Henry Picard, a gracious and helpful veteran who loaned both money and advice, and to Dutch Harrison.

Harrison discovered one evening when he was rooming with Ben just how determined the Texan was. Dutch couldn't go to sleep because Hogan kept beating his fists against the bedposts in their hotel room. "Have you gone crazy?" Dutch asked.

"I'm strengthening my wrists," said Hogan. . . .

FABULOUS FOURSOME Byron Nelson, Ben Hogan, Bobby Jones and Jimmy Demaret (clockwise from top right) reminisced at the '46 Masters.

1998 | LONG-DRIVE CHAMPION Jason Zuback generated 156-mph clubhead speed to smash 400-yard drives and the occasional phone book. | *Photograph by* TODD KOROL

LEADERS | TODAY | HOLE | TOTAL
STEWART | 1 | 13 | 4
AUSTIN | 2 | 10 | 1
MONTGOMERIE | 4 | 16 | 1
ELS | 4 | 11 | 2
JANZEN | 4 | 14 | 1
NORMAN | 1 | F | 1
NICKLAUS | | 15 |
GIBSON | 1 | 8 |
COOK | 1 | 8 | 1
CIN | | 4 |

1996 | ERNIE ELS, the Big Easy, had a hard time with a bunker's fat lip during the U.S. Open at Oakland Hills. | *Photograph by* JACQUELINE DUVOISIN

2003 | CAPT. JASON CONROY of the U.S. Army's 3rd Infantry Division tried Persian golf while stationed in Iraq. | *Photograph by* BRANT SANDERLIN

IT IS TIME TO ACKNOWLEDGE WHAT HAS become stupefyingly obvious: The tournament that used to be called the Crosby, after the great crooner Bing, has become, for all practical purposes, the Murray, after the man who last Friday gave a scalp massage to a female spectator on the 15th tee and hit the Pebble Beach sign above the golf shop with a well-flung banana. Bill Murray is a multisport comedian. He oversees promotions as co-owner of a couple of minor league baseball teams, and he's done play-by-play on a Cubs broadcast. But it's his annual appearances at the AT&T Pebble Beach National Pro-Am that provide spiritual refreshment.

On that hallowed, ocean-kissed course Murray plays golf like nobody else, but like golf was a game meant for playing. And people find this irresistible. At Pebble Beach even Tiger Woods gets eclipsed by *Caddyshack*'s Carl Spackler. How else to explain that advance ticket sales for this year, when Woods was out and Murray in, outstripped last year, when Murray missed but Tiger played?

You could call Murray the Meadowlark Lemon of golf, except the Globetrotters had more set pieces. Murray flies blind and flirts shamelessly. "Stick with us," he told two women on Friday. "Maybe we'll find some beer and wine." Later he scored a blue scarf from a female fan and wore it around his waist the rest of the round. When eight teenagers in sombreros joined his gallery, Murray cocked an eyebrow and said, "Are you here for the closing ceremonies?" Then he added, "I thought we tightened up our borders." Saturday was Murray's banana day: He tossed a peel at his pro partner, Scott Simpson, on the 1st tee, which incited Simpson and the rest of the foursome, actor Andy Garcia and pro Paul Stankowski, to throw bananas back. This is not, you see, a man who demands quiet on the course. "You!" Murray said suddenly, pointing to a white-haired woman watching him on the 10th tee last Thursday. "I need you in my posse!"

That's not exactly an exclusive group. The working-class kid from Wilmette, Ill., is the Pied Piper of Pebble Beach. Kevin Costner had 25 fans behind him as he came off the 14th tee on Thursday. Murray, playing just behind him, had at least 10 times that number.

What makes the scene even more delicious is that the golf establishment once opposed Murray's even being in the Murray. In their defense, PGA honchos circa 1992 were unprepared for a golfer wearing bib overalls and a hat shaped like the Hubert Humphrey Metrodome. . . .

2007 | THE CLOWN PRINCE of the pro-am, *Caddyshack* star Bill Murray kept a lid on his shenanigans while chasing down a putt at Pebble Beach. | *Photograph by* ROBERT BECK

1975 | UP–AND–COMER Tom Watson, 25, challenged at the U.S. Open before winning the first of his five British Opens a month later. | *Photograph by* USGA MUSEUM

1964 | THE GREAT GUNDY, JoAnne Gunderson, won five Women's Amateurs before shining as the LPGA's "Big Mama" JoAnne Carner. | *Photograph by* USGA MUSEUM

1997 | THE SPORTS world changed for good on the April afternoon when Tiger Woods won his first Masters. | *Photograph by* JOHN IACONO

SEARCHING FOR A SEA OF TRANQUILITY

BY STEVE WULF

Life was one big unplayable lie for Phil McGleno until he became the colorful, quotable, ambidextrous Mac O'Grady. Was Mac O. a wacko, a genius, or both?　　　—from SI, APRIL 16, 1984

WHEN HE WALKS DOWN the fairway, there is such joy in his step that the gallery can't help but notice. Someone will ask, "Who *is* that?" and a marshal will respond, "Mac O'Grady." "Who's he?" Good question. Mac O'Grady was 101st on the Professional Golfers' Association's money list last year, winning $50,379. There may have been a hundred better golfers on the Tour, but none of them had a better story than Mac O'Grady.

For one thing, he has two names, Mac O'Grady and Phillip McGleno. And with each name comes a different persona, a front side and a back side, so to speak. The Mac O'Grady known to most of his fellow touring pros is an irrepressible zany, one of golf's so-called Space Cadets. In fact, he has drafted a letter to NASA, volunteering his services to the space program. He wanted the '84 PGA media guide to list his special interest as molecular biology, but his request was made too late.

O'Grady is a switch-hitter, and he has applied to the USGA for amateur status as a lefthander. He has also taken applications from convicts all over the country who would like to be his caddie. Minnesota-born Mac speaks in a language, and in an accent, all his own—a wedge shot isn't just a wedge shot, but "a bird flying to the firmaments, outlined against an incandescent sky, beginning to fall, gently sashaying back to the earth." Crazy? Why, he went through the PGA qualifying school 17 times beginning in 1971 before finally winning his touring card in November of 1982.

But then there's Phil McGleno, who lived through a nightmare to chase his dream. Along the way, he found love and hate and friendship, shuttled between California, Texas, Florida, everywhere in Greyhound buses, devoured all manner of books, lived in a storage box in a garage, worked at the oddest of jobs, read more books and finally changed his name.

Persistent? Well, one 72-to-144-hole qualifying tournament is an ordeal. The thought of enduring 17 of them in 12 years boggles the mind.

So there were tears in his eyes as he walked down the 18th fairway of the Tournament Players Club course on Nov. 21, 1982, the last day of his last qualifying school. Phil McGleno had finally caught up with his dream. As he wrote in his journal that night, "A philosopher once stated, 'Your happiness in Life is measured by how deep sorrow has cut within you.' At this moment, we [he and his wife, Fumiko] are the happiest people in the universe. God bless those who move mountains."

There are all sorts of pleasures to be had in listening to O'Grady's husky voice. "Anytime you talk to him, you'll hear three words you never heard before," says fellow pro Mike Nicolette. O'Grady is liable to babble on, hooking words out-of-bounds, slicing the language into the trees, but he says things with such abandon that he will stop every once in a while to laugh at himself.

"It's that high-pitched laugh that gets me," says Bill Kratzert, another pro. "Even when I can't understand what he's saying, I'll laugh at the laugh." O'Grady also speaks with a lilt that comes from some undiscovered land. But this is understandable, given that his wife is Japanese, his friends could form their own United Nations, and the man who supported him through many lean years is called Raphael Shapiro, which isn't the name *he* was born with.

Just watching O'Grady can be a treat. It's not that he's handsome—his cheeks are drawn and his nose is pinched—but rather it's the way he carries himself. He is so full of energy that he literally runs from point to point. At 32, he's in such good shape that many golfers consider him to be the best-conditioned athlete on the Tour. He neither smokes nor drinks.

On the course, his swing is also something to behold. "He has the best mechanics out here," says Gary McCord, another Space Cadet. Remarkably, O'Grady has the same swing from the other side. During a practice round before the Bing Crosby Pro-Am in February, he turned his righthanded driver backwards and drove the ball lefthanded—250 yards and dead down the middle of the 18th fairway at Pebble Beach. . . .

A QUIXOTIC QUEST to make a name for himself on the PGA Tour found O'Grady wading in against golf's conformist tide.

SI'S ALLTIME GREATEST GOLFERS

The IMMORTALS' INVITATIONAL

PHOTO ILLUSTRATION BY AARON GOODMAN

WOULD TIGER BEAT the Golden Bear in golf's ultimate big-game battle? Is Tiger Woods's dominance over the past 13 years a greater feat than Jack Nicklaus's over 25 years? While we're at it, who had the better career, Sam Snead or Arnold Palmer? Annika Sorenstam or Old Tom Morris? Who's to say? ॐ We assembled a stellar blue-ribbon panel to say. Each of our expert judges listed his or her top 20 golfers of all time, in order. Panelists were free to consider on-course achievements only or to factor in character or other contributions, as they saw fit. Players got 20 points for each first-place vote, 19 for second and so on, down to one point for a 20th-place vote. The results are sure to start arguments. ॐ

With 15 judges, 300 points was the maximum. Nicklaus, with 290 points, and Woods, with 283, came close. Bobby Jones collected 265. Almost every panelist put those three players at the top: Beyond that towering threesome only Ben Hogan, Snead and Palmer got a single Top 3 vote. Byron Nelson, Mickey Wright, Sorenstam, Young Tom Morris and Babe Didrikson Zaharias all received at least one 4th-place vote, but three of them finished outside the Top 10. Nicklaus's rivals Lee Trevino—who tossed Jack a toy snake before their 1971 U.S. Open playoff—and Billy Casper snagged two of the last three spots. ॐ Who missed the cut? Nick Faldo (34 points) with his six majors fell just short of No. 20 Casper with his three. Next came Peter Thomson (28), Greg Norman (27), Kathy Whitworth (26), James Braid and J.H. Taylor (tied at 16) and Phil Mickelson (15). Francis Ouimet rounded out the voting with a single point. ॐ Let the arguments begin.

THE JUDGES

TIM FINCHEM, *Commissioner, PGA Tour* ॐ DAVID FAY, *Executive Director, USGA*

PETER DAWSON, *Chief Executive, Royal and Ancient Golf Club of St. Andrews* ॐ CAROLYN BIVENS, *Commissioner, LPGA*

JOE STERANKA, *CEO, PGA of America* ॐ JACK PETER, *COO, World Golf Hall of Fame*

DOUG FERGUSON, *President, Golf Writers Association of America* ॐ RAND JERRIS, *Director, USGA Communications and Museum*

DEANE BEMAN, *Former Commissioner, PGA Tour* ॐ JAMES P. HERRE, *Golf Editor, Sports Illustrated*

DAVID CLARKE, *Editor, Golf Magazine* ॐ MICHAEL BAMBERGER, *Senior Writer, Sports Illustrated*

ALAN SHIPNUCK, *Senior Writer, Sports Illustrated* ॐ GARY VAN SICKLE, *Senior Writer, Sports Illustrated*

JOHN GARRITY, *Special Contributor, Sports Illustrated*

TOM WATSON

BEN HOGAN

GENE SARAZEN

SAM SNEAD

HARRY VARDON

MICKEY WRIGHT   OLD TOM MORRIS   ARNOLD PALMER

WALTER HAGEN   TIGER WOODS

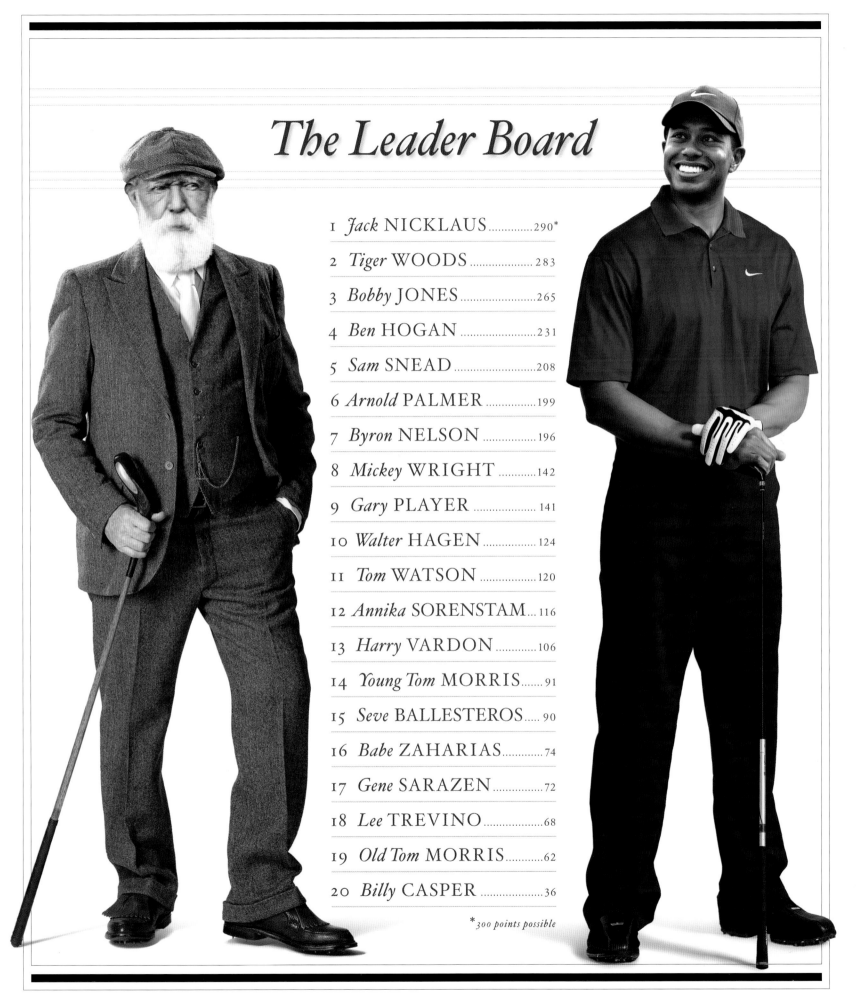

The Leader Board

1 *Jack* NICKLAUS.............290*

2 *Tiger* WOODS...................283

3 *Bobby* JONES....................265

4 *Ben* HOGAN.......................231

5 *Sam* SNEAD.......................208

6 *Arnold* PALMER................199

7 *Byron* NELSON.................196

8 *Mickey* WRIGHT............142

9 *Gary* PLAYER...................141

10 *Walter* HAGEN................124

11 *Tom* WATSON..................120

12 *Annika* SORENSTAM...116

13 *Harry* VARDON...........106

14 *Young Tom* MORRIS.......91

15 *Seve* BALLESTEROS.....90

16 *Babe* ZAHARIAS...........74

17 *Gene* SARAZEN...............72

18 *Lee* TREVINO.................68

19 *Old Tom* MORRIS...........62

20 *Billy* CASPER...................36

300 points possible

ANNIKA SORENSTAM   BABE ZAHARIAS   LEE TREVINO

SEVE BALLESTEROS   JACK NICKLAUS

BILLY CASPER   YOUNG TOM MORRIS   BOBBY JONES   BYRON NELSON   GARY PLAYER

> ## Celebrities

Marquee Players

A pastime once enjoyed by British royalty proved irresistible to modern stars male and female

1961 | JACQUELINE KENNEDY · 2007 | HEATHER LOCKLEAR · 1935 | KATHARINE HEPBURN

2008 | ELLEN DeGENERES · 1964 | DORIS DAY · 2005 | CATHERINE ZETA-JONES

1962 | THE NEWLY anointed Bond, Scotland's Sean Connery, proved to be more than a match for golf foe Goldfinger. | *Photograph by* CHRIS WARE

1971 | ROUGHING IT at Royal Birkdale, Tony Jacklin slipped further behind eventual British Open champion Lee Trevino. | *Photograph by* GERRY CRANHAM

1999 | WITH NO stance and no backswing, Craig Parry ditched strategy in favor of the old hit 'n' hope at the British Open. | *Photograph by* HEINZ KLUETMEIER

1955 - 1969

The Rise *of* Arnie *and* Jack

RUNNER-UP AND CHAMPION
Nicklaus wins the U.S. Open
1962
Photograph by JOHN DOMINIS

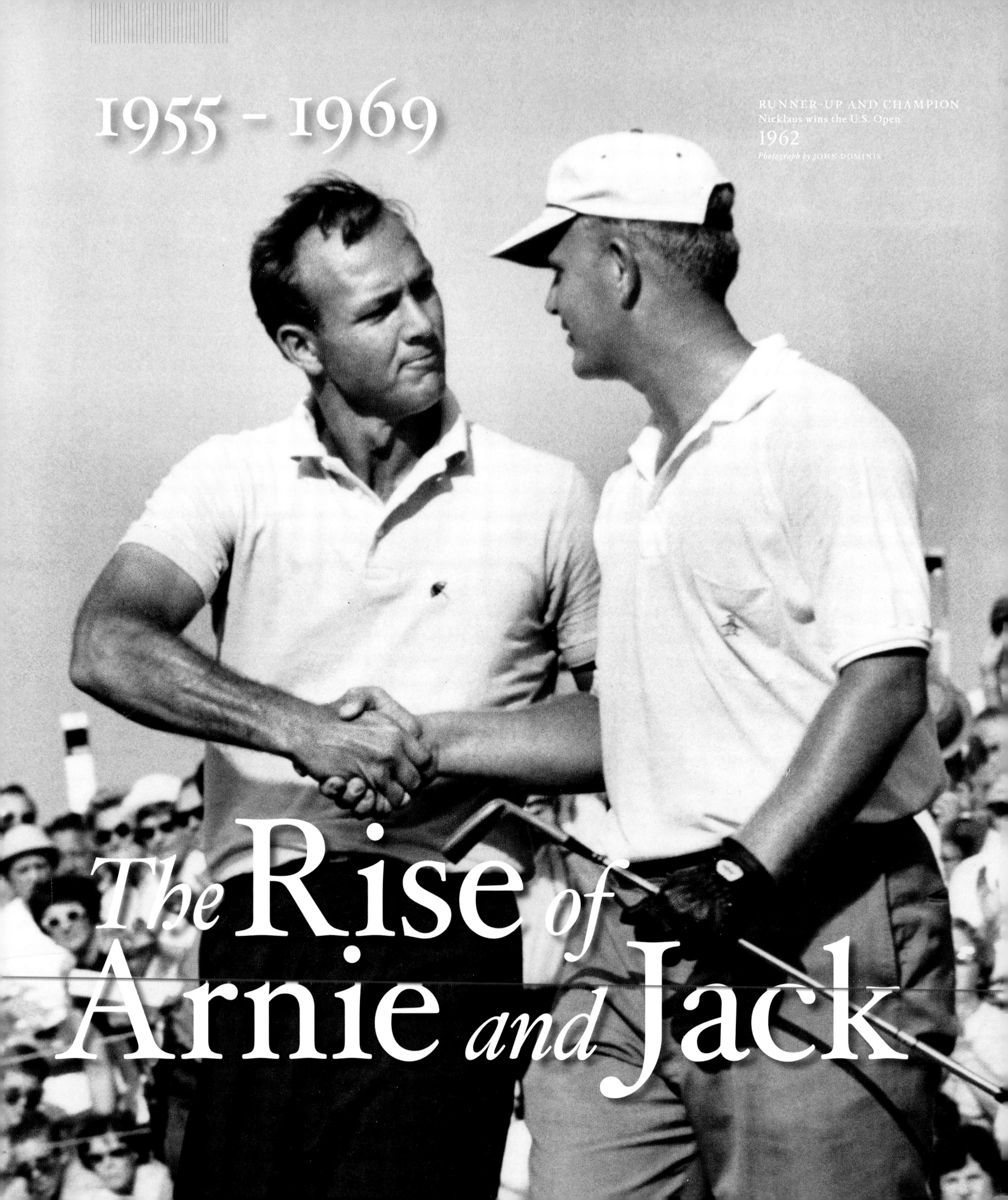

THE ERA'S BEST

Jack Nicklaus

The two-time U.S. Amateur champion from Ohio State finished second to Arnold Palmer in the 1960 U.S. Open and went on to rack up 11 majors in the next dozen years.

Arnold Palmer

Leading Arnie's Army by acclamation, the charismatic son of a greenkeeper won seven majors and drew millions of fans to the sport just as TV turned its lens toward the golf course.

Mickey Wright

With a swing admired by Ben Hogan and Byron Nelson, San Diego's Mary Kathryn Wright collected 13 majors in less than a decade (1958–66) and a total of 82 LPGA titles.

Gary Player

The fitness pioneer won the Masters and British Open three times each and added two PGA Championships and a U.S. Open while promoting the game around the world.

Roberto De Vicenzo

The luckless star from Argentina is remembered more for signing an incorrect scorecard at the 1968 Masters than for his 231 victories worldwide, including the '67 British Open.

>MILESTONES<

1955
GREG NORMAN
Born February 10

1956
BABE DIDRIKSON ZAHARIAS
Dies at age 45

1957
NICK FALDO
Born July 18

1961
GARY PLAYER
First foreign-born Masters champ

1962
JACK NICKLAUS
Pro debut at Los Angeles Open

1965
PGA Q SCHOOL
Held for the first time

1966
BRITISH OPEN
Goes from three to four days

1968
ARNOLD PALMER
First golfer to earn $1 million

1969
WALTER HAGEN >
Dies at age 76

1969
ERNIE ELS
Born October 17

NOW OPEN FOR PLAY

Hazeltine National
CHASKA, MINNESOTA
1962 / Designed by Robert Trent Jones
< THE 16TH HUGS LAKE HAZELTINE ON A COURSE INFAMOUS FOR ITS DOGLEGS AND BLIND SHOTS.

Bellerive
CREVE COEUR, MISSOURI
1959 / Robert Trent Jones

Spyglass Hill
PEBBLE BEACH, CALIFORNIA
1966 / Robert Trent Jones

Harbour Town
HILTON HEAD, SOUTH CAROLINA
1969 / Pete Dye & Jack Nicklaus

>> GOLF IN THE REAL WORLD <<

Golf Honeymoon October 15, 1955 *Honeymooners* antihero Ralph Kramden, played by avid golfer Jackie Gleason, learns the game from neighbor Ed Norton (Art Carney) in hopes of impressing his boss and landing a promotion. Upon reading that a golfer must address the ball, Norton recites the classic line, "Hello, ball!"

Burbank Shot October 1, 1962 Tennis enthusiast Johnny Carson > takes over as host of *The Tonight Show* and soon begins panto-miming a golf swing at the end of his monologue, supposedly hitting the ball to Doc Severinsen and the show's band. The move becomes iconic, and over the years many of Carson's guest hosts imitate the swing. But during the last of his 4,531 shows, in '92, Johnny leaves the phantom club in the imaginary bag.

Studying Arnie's Line August 7, 1960 Immediately after winning the Insurance City Open in Hartford, Arnold Palmer hurries to New York to appear on the game show *What's My Line?* Bennett Cerf is the only one of four panelists to identify Palmer as a pro golfer.

A Barrier Broken April 13, 1961 Charlie Sifford, a former Army infantryman and personal golf coach to singer Billy Eckstine, becomes the first African-American golfer to receive a tour card after the PGA reverses its notorious "Caucasians-only" clause. Sifford's first appearance as a PGA member comes at the Greater Greensboro Open, where under intense scrutiny he ties for fourth behind winner Mike Souchak, earning $1,300.

Golden Rulebreaker January 9, 1965 Agent 007 and criminal mastermind Auric Goldfinger play a match at Royal St. George's (actually Stoke Poges Golf Club in England) in the third James Bond film, and Bond catches Goldfinger cheating. After the villain's razor-sharp caddie, Oddjob, drops a ball down his pantleg, Bond's caddie says, "If that's his original ball, I'm Arnold Palmer."

A golfer trudged down a riverside fairway in a storm. Seeing two men sitting by the river, he muttered, "Look at those idiots fishing in the rain."

BEST SHOT

JULY 30, 1961

Jerry Barber

Down by two strokes with three holes to play at the PGA Championship, Barber caps his comeback by rolling in a 60-foot birdie putt at the final hole, forcing a playoff with Don January that Barber wins.

WORST SHOT

APRIL 10, 1961

Arnold Palmer

Needing an up-and-down from the right-front bunker on 18 to claim his second straight green jacket, Palmer sails his third shot over the green and down a swale. The chip and two putts that follow give Gary Player the title.

> THE SWING *With his unique and powerful lash at the ball, popular* ARNOLD PALMER *swung hard and finished high.*

> GOLF EVOLVES

MAKING PAR In 1956 the USGA establishes the current parameters for par: Holes up to 250 yards are designated as par-3s; those from 251 to 470 yards are par-4s and holes longer than 471 are par-5s. From now on, all par-6s are unofficial.

NEW RULES In a series of 1960 rule-book changes, the USGA allows lifting, cleaning and replacing balls on putting surfaces, creating a need for the first ball markers. Also imposed by the new regulations: a limit of one caddie per golfer.

BELLY PUTTERS Though it won't catch on until Paul Azinger uses one in 1999, the belly putter is patented in '65 and used on Tour by Phil Rogers in '68. Traditionalists still have their doubts about the club.

CROQUET STYLE Sam Snead first tries it as a cure for his yips—putting while standing perpendicular to the target line. Such sidewinding is outlawed in 1968.

GAME CHANGER: CAVITY BACKS
Ping founder Karsten Solheim realized that spreading weight around the perimeter of the clubhead would enlarge the sweet spot. Presto—a more forgiving club. Ping brought out its new K Series irons in 1969.

>> FROM THE VAULT

"LAST NIGHT I HAD some real good eatin'. I went out in the woods back of my house there in Hot Springs and shot me a couple of nice fat squirrels. Took 'em home and skinned 'em and then parboiled 'em. Fried 'em up with some apple slices, and I tell you there's no better eatin' in this world."

—SAM SNEAD'S FRIED-SQUIRREL RECIPE, *in* SI, DECEMBER 12, 1960

> ON THE NUMBER

2 Aces by Bill Whedon on the front nine during the first round of the 1955 Insurance City Open. Whedon is the only Tour player to make two holes in one in a single nine.

13 Victories by Mickey Wright during the 1963 season, an LPGA record that still stands.

$31,269 Wright's total earnings in 1963.

8 Consecutive birdies by Bob Goalby during the 1961 St. Petersburg Open, which he won. Five others have since equaled the feat.

39 Consecutive Bing Crosby Pro-Am appearances by Charlie Seaver, including a one-stroke triumph in the '64 Clambake. Seaver, a food-industry executive credited with the idea of adding raisins to cereal, is better known as the father of baseball Hall of Famer Tom Seaver.

48 Age of Julius Boros when he won the PGA Championship at Pecan Valley in 1968, making him the oldest player to win a major.

257 Score for Mike Souchak at the '55 Texas Open, a record 27 under par. Souchak's mark stood for 46 years, until Mark Calcavecchia went 28 under at the 2001 Phoenix Open.

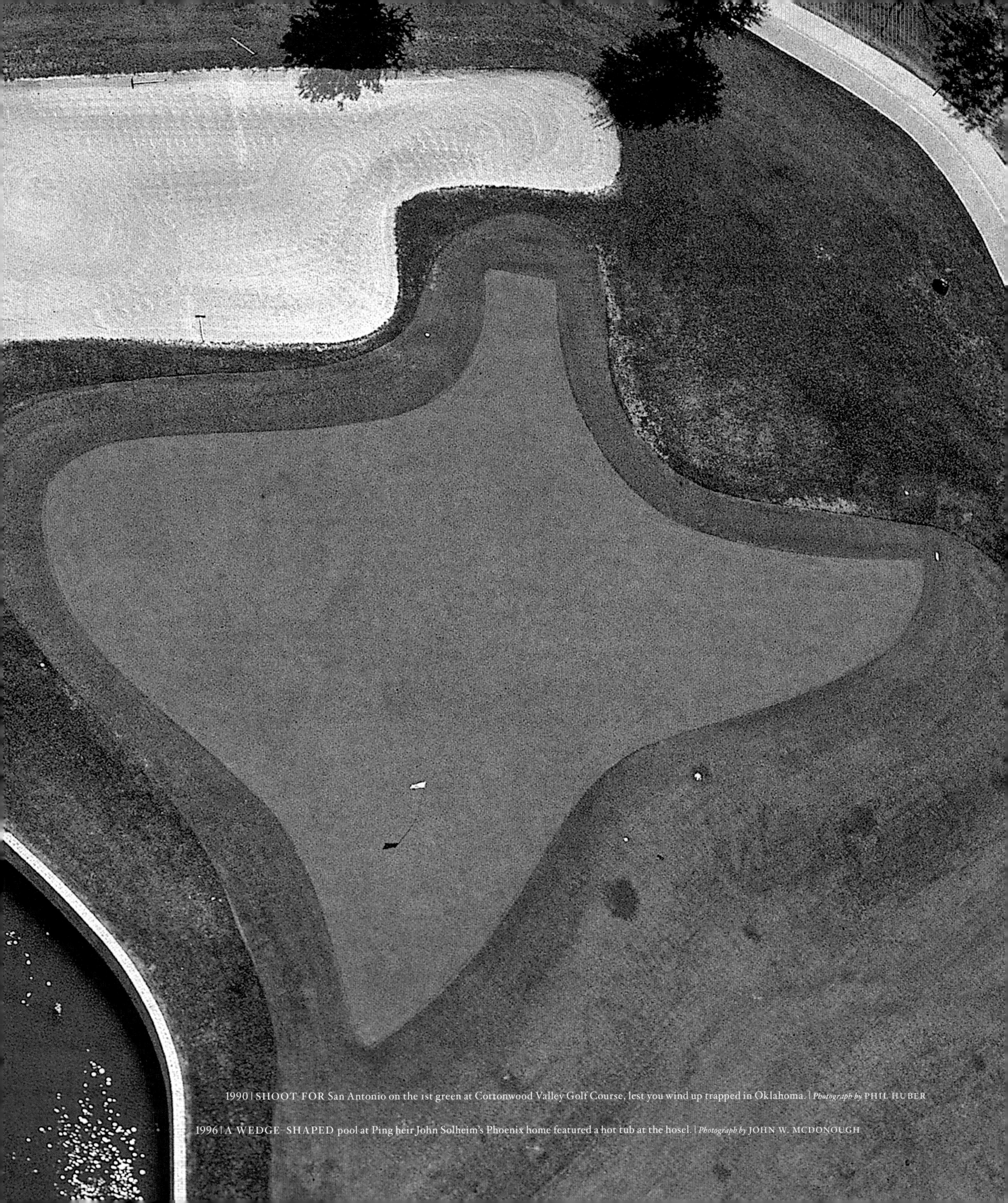

1990 | SHOOT FOR San Antonio on the 1st green at Cottonwood Valley Golf Course, lest you wind up trapped in Oklahoma. | *Photograph by* PHIL HUBER

1996 | A WEDGE-SHAPED pool at Ping heir John Solheim's Phoenix home featured a hot tub at the hosel. | *Photograph by* JOHN W. MCDONOUGH

THERE'S NEVER BEEN AN OPEN LIKE IT

BY DAN JENKINS

Past, present and future came together one day in 1960 as Arnold Palmer chased Ben Hogan and Jack Nicklaus. —*from* SI, JUNE 19, 1978

THEY WERE THE MOST astonishing four hours in golf since Mary, Queen of Scots found out what dormie meant and invented the back nine. And now, given 18 years of reflection, they still seem as significant to the game as, for instance, the day Arnold Palmer began hitching up his trousers, or the moment Jack Nicklaus decided to thin down and let his hair fluff, or that interlude in the pro shop when Ben Hogan selected his first white cap.

Small wonder that no sportswriter was capable of outlining it against a bright blue summer sky and letting the four adjectives ride again: It was too big, too wildly exciting, too crazily suspenseful, too suffocatingly dramatic. What exactly happened? Oh, not much. Just a routine collision of three decades at one historical intersection.

On that afternoon, in the span of just 18 holes, we witnessed the arrival of Nicklaus, the coronation of Palmer and the end of Hogan. Nicklaus was a 20-year-old amateur who would own the 1970s. Palmer was a 30-year-old pro who would dominate the 1960s. Hogan was a 47-year-old immortal who had overwhelmed the 1950s. While they had a fine supporting cast, it was primarily these three men who waged war for the U.S. Open championship on that Saturday of June 18, 1960. The battle was continuous, under a steaming Colorado sun at Cherry Hills Country Club in Denver. In those days there was something in sport known as Open Saturday. It is no longer a part of golf, thanks to television—no thanks, actually. But it was a day like no other; a day on which the best golfers in the world were required to play 36 holes because it had always seemed to the USGA that a prolonged test of physical and mental stamina should go into the earning of the game's most important title. Thus, Open Saturday lent itself to wondrous comebacks and horrendous collapses, and it provided a full day's ration of every emotion familiar to the athlete competing under pressure for a prize so important as to be beyond the comprehension of most people.

Open Saturday had been an institution with the USGA since its fourth annual championship in 1898. There had been thrillers before 1960, Saturdays that had tested the Bobby Joneses, Walter Hagens, Gene Sarazens, Harry Vardons, Francis Ouimets, Byron Nelsons, Sam Sneads—and, of course, the Ben Hogans—not to forget the occasional unknowns like John L. Black, Roland Hancock and Lee Mackey, all of them performing in wonderfully predictable and unexpectedly horrible ways, and so writing the history of the game in that one event, the National Open.

But any serious scholar of the sport, or anyone fortunate enough to have been there at Cherry Hills, is aware that the Open Saturday of Arnold, Ben and Jack was something very special—a U.S. Open that in meaning for the game continues to dwarf all of the others.

The casual fan will remember 1960 as the year old Arnie won when he shot a 65 in the last round and became the real Arnold Palmer. Threw his visor in the air, smoked a bunch of cigarettes, chipped in, drove a ball through a tree trunk, tucked in his shirttail, and lived happily ever after with Winnie and President Eisenhower.

And that is pretty much what happened. But there is a constant truth about tournament golf: Other men have to lose a championship before one man can win it. And never has the final 18 of an Open produced as many losers as Cherry Hills did in 1960. When it was over, there were as many stretcher cases as there were shouts of "Whoo-ha, go get 'em, Arnie!" And that stood to reason after you considered that in those insane four hours Palmer came from seven strokes off the lead. . . .

ARNOLD WAS cursing the 1st hole, a 346-yard par-4 with an elevated tee. Three times he had just missed driving the green. As he left the group to join Paul Harney for their 1:42 starting time on the final 18, the thing on his mind was trying to drive that 1st green. It would be his one Cherry Hills accomplishment.

"If I drive the green and get a birdie or an eagle, I might shoot 65," Palmer said. "What'll that do?"

[Writer Bob] Drum said, "Nothing. You're too far back."

"It would give me 280," Palmer said. "Doesn't 280 always win the Open?"

"Yeah, when Hogan shoots it," Drum said. . . .

AFTER DRIVING the 1st green at Cherry Hills, Palmer charged like a man possessed, then holed the winning putt and flung his visor skyward.

1930s | CLUBHEADS MET knuckleheads when the Fore Stooges goofed on a Hollywood green. | *Photograph by* MOVIE STILL ARCHIVES

1959 | NEWLY VICTORIOUS revolutionaries Che Guevara (putting) and Fidel Castro teed it up in Havana. | *Photograph by* ALBERTO KORDA

1987 | LARRY MIZE rose to the occasion by holing a 140-foot chip to shock Greg Norman in their Masters playoff. | *Photograph by* JOHN IACONO

1991 | IAN WOOSNAM of Wales, all 64½ inches of him, whaled his drives and sank this seven-foot putt to nab the green jacket. | *Photograph by* JOHN IACONO

SAM SNEAD AND THE SERPENT

BY GERALD HOLLAND

Slammin' Sam Snead possessed the sweetest swing in creation. He feared no reptile and played a swingin' trumpet too.

—*from* SI, DECEMBER 5, 1960

SAM SNEAD GROANED ALOUD. "There's too much of this runnin' around. Hollywood yesterday, Washington tomorrow, back to Hollywood next day. Man, I tell you, when I git enough money ahead, I'm goin' to take things easy. I won't even take a lick at a snake. Some ol' snake comes after me, I'm goin' to say, 'Git along there, snake! Go on now, don't bother me. Go chew on somebody else.'"

Now, in the Appalachian mountain country of Virginia where Sam Snead was born and raised, any man who lets a rattler or a copperhead slither by without taking a whack at it has definitely attained the height of laziness.

Sam Snead spoke of his long-range intentions toward snakes one recent evening in Boston. Sam was very weary at the time. But not too many evenings later, after flying to Hollywood and back and then taking the time to catch up on his sleep, he stood on a bandstand in White Sulphur Springs, W.Va., bright-eyed and bubbling over with high spirits as he happily sang:

"Heart of my heart,

I love that melodee-e-e-e-e!"

"Sing it, Sambo!" cried the crowd on the dance floor at The Pines, a little nightclub near the celebrated Greenbrier, Sam's home course.

"Heart of my heart," bellowed Sam. "Brings back a *memoree-e-e-e*!"

"That's it, that's it, Sam!" shrilled Miss Ellie, a fine buxom hostess enjoying a night off from the plush Colonial Club down the line. "You're right on the beam!"

The bald-headed man on the bandstand, considered by many of his admirers to be the greatest golfer the professional game has ever known, threw back his head and roared on.

"When we were kids on the corner of the square. . .we were rough and ready guys. . .but, Oh-H-H how we could *har-mon-ize*!"

"Let's hear that horn, Sam!"

Sam raised his trumpet to his lips and the Four Populaires (Bill Sloane at the piano, Bill Walz on the bass, Chuck Bills on the sax and Kenny Martin on the trombone) plus Freddie Leach at the vibraphone, Howard Harvey on the cornet and Gary Nixon on the clarinet all joined in. The Four Populaires entertain in the Old White Club at the Greenbrier. Freddie Leach is with the Meyer Davis orchestra that plays in the Greenbrier's main dining room. Howard Harvey and his wife Betty dance as a team in the Old White Club and Gary Nixon is Sam Snead's assistant.

The hour was 2 a.m. Sam had retired early, but when the professional musicians were sitting around having coffee after their work was done about midnight, somebody suggested a jam session. It was then I remembered for the first time (I had been traveling around with him for almost a month) that Sam Snead played a trumpet and, moreover, he carried a union musician's card. I remarked that I'd give just about anything in this world to hear Sam Snead cut loose with a few wails on the horn.

"Well, shucks, man," exclaimed Bill Sloane, the piano player. "That's easy. Let's wake 'im up and go on down to The Pines."

"Oh, no sir!" I said, shaking my head emphatically. "I've come to know this man Snead over the past month. I've been with him in Boston, Providence, Washington, Rockville, Md., Hollywood, Hot Springs, Va., and right here in White Sulphur. And I tell you, boys, that man can get mighty peevish and downright mean and sassy when he is deprived of his proper rest."

Bill Sloane gave me a long look. "Mister," he said, "you may have been all those places and you may have observed Mr. Sam Snead in many different circumstances, but. . . ."

I interrupted. "Including many hours on the golf course. I saw him play Arnold Palmer twice, and various other celebrities, big movie stars in Hollywood and so on, and he never shot out of the 60s once—not once! Palmer himself says Snead is playing better than he ever did. I attribute that to his getting his proper rest wherever possible—and I say to you, wake him up at this hour of the night and he'll give you a chewing out you won't forget.". . .

A LEGENDARY athlete who won bets by leaping and touching clubhouse ceilings with his toe, Snead hurdled a hedge at a late-'30s tournament.

1985 | A LIP-OUT left Bernhard Langer in limbo during a Masters he would win thanks to Curtis Strange's stumbles. | *Photograph by* JACQUELINE DUVOISIN

1997 | FOUR-TIME Tour winner Billy Andrade couldn't shoulder the agony every golfer feels when the cup dodges a good putt. | *Photograph by* ROBERT BECK

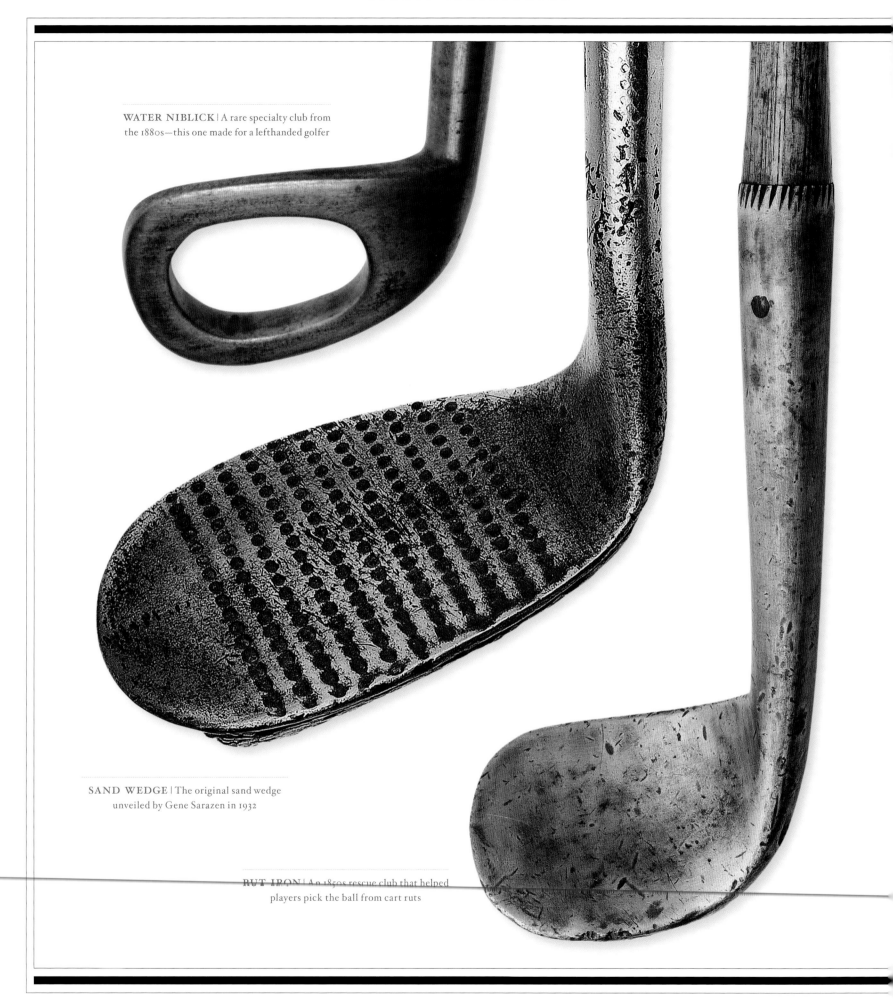

WATER NIBLICK | A rare specialty club from
the 1880s—this one made for a lefthanded golfer

SAND WEDGE | The original sand wedge
unveiled by Gene Sarazen in 1932

RUT IRON | An 1850s rescue club that helped
players pick the ball from cart ruts

> **Artifacts**

Tools of the Trade

Centuries after a shepherd's crook evolved into woods and cleeks like these, and half a century after Winston Churchill groused that the game is "played with weapons singularly ill-suited to the purpose," the search for the perfect club continues. . .

PUTTER | Square shooter made around 1915 by
Jean Gassiat, the Scotty Cameron of his day

PLAY CLUB | Willie Park, the first British Open
winner, carved this ancestor of the driver

DAVID N. BERKWITZ, WORLD GOLF HALL OF FAME (4) AND USGA MUSEUM (SAND WEDGE)

A 1,000-TO-1 SHOT

BY DAN JENKINS

Jack Nicklaus could barely believe the chip Tom Watson sank to win the U.S. Open at Pebble Beach's 17th. —from SI, JUNE 28, 1982

FROM WHERE TOM WATSON WAS on the 71st hole of the U.S. Open golf championship Sunday at Pebble Beach—in the garbage, on a downslope, looking at a slick green—you don't simply chip the ball into the cup for a birdie to beat Jack Nicklaus, who is already in the scorer's tent with a total good enough to win. First, you throw up.

Well, that's wrong, of course. If you're Watson, by now you're accustomed to beating Nicklaus in major tournaments because you've done it before at the Masters and in the British Open, so you lay open the blade of a sand wedge and plop the lob-chip shot softly onto the putting surface and then watch the flagstick get in the way of the ball to keep it from running all the way to the Lodge.

Of the many dramatic and championship-twisting shots that were struck and misstruck all last week on the Monterey Peninsula, and in all of the 81 Opens that came before this one, Watson's chip-in at the 17th on Sunday will be remembered for as long as men sew leather patches on the elbows of their tweed jackets.

Two quotes must be pressed into the family Bible along with the 16-foot hole-out that gave Watson his first Open title and his sixth major. Watson's regular caddie, Bruce Edwards, said to him before the shot, "Get it close." Replied Watson, "I'm not gonna get it close, I'm gonna make it!"

This was why Watson could be seen pointing at someone (Edwards) as he went into that sprint and dance around the edge of the green after the ball darted into the cup. If he had been a little more delirious and a little less careful, he might have discoed right into Carmel Bay.

Which brings up quote No. 2. Nicklaus was watching Watson's progress on a TV monitor in back of the 18th green. He had shot a fourth-round 69, three under par, and had a total of 284, four under for the 72 holes—six strokes better than the 290 with which he had won the Open at Pebble Beach back in '72. He had seen Watson's less-than-perfect two-iron from the 17th tee bounce and find the high grass on the upslope to the left of the green.

Certain bogey, Jack thought; I win. . . . Nicklaus took his eyes off the monitor for just a second, and the next thing he saw on it was Watson looking like a man with an incurable itch, and a mighty roar was filling the air. A few minutes later, Watson was making a needless birdie at 18 to win by two strokes, and Nicklaus was shaking Tom's hand on the green, saying with a smile, "You little son of a bitch, you're something else."

So ended one of the more fantastic U.S. Opens, or majors, of recent years. In the end, it was another Watson-Nicklaus saga. *Watson–Nicklaus III*, check your local neighborhood theater. Number I came at Augusta in 1977, when Tom outbattled Jack in the stretch to win the first of his two Masters titles—with a birdie at the 17th, incidentally. No. II came later that summer at Turnberry in Scotland when Watson captured the second of his three British Open trophies in a furious head-to-head duel, 65–65 in the third round, then 65–66 in the last round, the decisive birdie again coming at the 17th hole. Now this at Pebble Beach, and on Pebble's picturesque 17th.

Watson's chip-in must rank in history with two similar shots that have more or less decided major championships, although Watson's no doubt is the most stunning of the three. There is the wedge Arnold Palmer holed out from beside the 16th green at the 1962 Masters, a stroke that enabled him to gain a playoff with Gary Player and Dow Finsterwald, which he won. Then there was the chip shot Lee Trevino sank on the next-to-last hole at Muirfield in the 1972 British Open, and Nicklaus, who was shooting for the third leg of a Grand Slam, also was the victim there—on the 17th, of course.

"Yes, it has happened to me before, but I didn't think it would happen again," Nicklaus said. . . . "I rate Tom's [shot] up there with Trevino's," he added. "I suppose I've done it to other people too. Maybe not by chipping in. When you think you've won, it's disappointing."

Of the shot, it was said by Bill Rogers, who was playing with Watson and wound up tied for third, that a man could drop the ball on the edge of the 17th green with his hand and it wouldn't stop short of the cup, so fast was the green. Then Rogers went on, "You could hit that chip a hundred times and you couldn't get it close to the pin, much less in the hole."

"A thousand times," said Nicklaus.

Watson and Rogers had begun the last round in a tie for the lead with Nicklaus three strokes back. There were other characters in the drama, but they would fade away, as is the case on major Sundays. . . .

FROM THE HAY above the hole, Watson threw one of history's epic haymakers at Nicklaus, the game's heavyweight champ.

2000 | KARRIE WEBB struck one straight and flush at the Australian Ladies Masters, seeking an ace in the hole. | *Photograph by* DARREN ENGLAND

2004 | TIGER WOODS got plenty of carry from the ultimate elevated tee, a helipad at Dubai's Burj Al Arab Hotel. | *Photograph by* DAVID CANNON

> Artifacts

Card Game

The same scorecard that attests to your genius if you break 60 could also break your heart

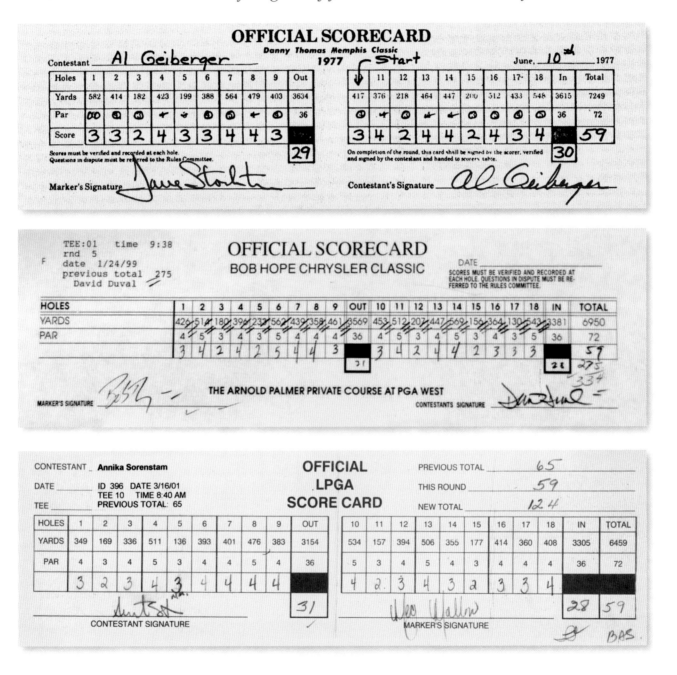

AL GEIBERGER carded the first 59 in Tour history in 1977 and David Duval the latest in '99, two years before Annika Sorenstam fired the LPGA's one and only 59.

1968 | ROBERTO DE VICENZO cost himself the Masters by signing for a 66 instead of the 65 he'd shot, then said, "What a stupid I am!" | *Photograph by* NEIL LEIFER

2007 | CARLOS FRANCO of Paraguay avoided a penalty stroke at Pebble Beach but had his week abridged when he missed the cut. | *Photograph by* ROBERT BECK

1999 | THREE SHOTS ahead with a hole to play at the British Open, Jean Van de Velde found himself up a creek called Barry Burn. | *Photograph by* ROSS KINNAIRD

CALL BACK THE YEARS

BY WILLIAM OSCAR JOHNSON

Our account of Charlie Sifford's landmark victory in the '69 L.A. Open was told in a late-Sixties style that reflected changing times.
—from SI, MARCH 31, 1969

THERE HE STOOD, PREPARING to address the crowd at the Black Fox in Los Angeles: Charles Luther Sifford, golfer, born 46 years ago in North Carolina, the son of a factory hand. His friends, soul brothers and sisters all, had gathered to laud him and applaud him, and to bring gifts to Charlie Sifford at the Black Fox, which is a nightclub cool and smoky located among the white man's oil wells, with Beverly Hills on one horizon and Watts on another. It was a rare occasion, for this day—Feb. 3—had been proclaimed Charlie Sifford Day throughout Los Angeles. The banks did not close for it, but there had been a small, spirited parade for Charlie—11 newly washed cars purring up 103rd Street, which was dubbed Charcoal Alley during the riots of 1965. Earlier Charlie had gone downtown to City Hall where the mayor of L.A., Sam Yorty, had jovially greeted him as "Mister Charlie," which broke everyone up. And as a sort of topper to the ceremonial part of it all, the Watts Chamber of Commerce announced that he, Charlie Sifford, a Negro who struck it rich in the white athlete's field of professional golf and who had just won the town's own Los Angeles Open, was to be the first man inducted into the Watts Hall of Fame.

Even though he is ordinarily a laconic man given to solemn consumption of an endless supply of large cigars, when Charlie squinted out at the people gathered in the Black Fox that night, he seemed quite moved. "It's just so wonderful to think that a black man can take a golf club and become so famous," he said. His friends applauded, then Charlie added quietly, "I just wish I could call back 10 years."

Charlie Sifford had spoken the truth: He had taken a golf club and he had become famous. Even quite rich. The capstone to his success, so far, was his $20,000 victory in the Los Angeles Open. The fact that Charlie Sifford happened to beat Harold Henning who happened to be a product (if not necessarily a practitioner) of South African apartheid was not lost on American black men. Negro newspapers were calling Charlie Sifford the epitome of Black Is Beautiful. Intrepid white reporters were making him uncomfortable (and uncooperative) by pressing him for quotes on everything racial from Nat Turner's confession to Muhammad Ali's conviction. His mail was up to 200 letters a week, a lot of it from Negro kids who lug bags around the nation's golf courses and dream about making it themselves in a sport that has never before had very much of a place for them.

Oh, the mantle of fame is upon Charlie Sifford; he is a celebrity in 1969, no doubt. Yet in a sadder but more significant sense, Charlie Sifford is just a survivor, a man of stamina and strong will who simply stayed on his feet while others fell. If ever a medal of solid gold is struck in the likeness of Charlie Sifford (and it must include that rocket of a cigar in his mouth) it will be to honor more his endurance than his victories, more his persistence than the brilliance of his game. He managed to outlive, outwait and, in a way, outgolf the years of Jim Crow in the Professional Golfers Association.

It was not until November 1961, when Charlie Sifford was a vintage 38-year-old and other major sports had long since been integrated, that the PGA moved to wipe out its regulation restricting membership to "professional golfers of the Caucasian race," and thus opened all of its tournaments to blacks. The PGA did not generate this action out of some intrinsic insight into the family of man (or even into the fraternity of golf). It did not act, in fact, until the attorney general of California had, quite publicly and quite legally, humiliated the association. The attorney general then was one Stanley Mosk, who later became celebrated for his scathing description of the John Birch Society as "little old ladies in tennis shoes." In 1961 he treated the doughty PGA as if it were simply a little old lady in golf shoes by forcing it to move its forthcoming national championship right out of Los Angeles and off to the Aronimink Golf Club, Newtown Square, Pa. Grounds for the eviction were that racial discrimination as practiced by the PGA did not jibe with the sovereign laws of California. Stanley Mosk has always been remembered by blacks for his part in that episode: The day after Sifford won the L.A. Open this year, a telegram arrived at Mosk's home. It said: "Thank you for opening the door for the Charlie Siffords of this world."

Of course, there is only one Charlie Sifford of this world and if Mosk's action opened the door for him, it was Charlie's own determination and patience that widened the gate. . . .

FOR SIFFORD, a six-time National Negro Open champion, victory on the PGA Tour was as sweet as sneaking a putt in the side door.

2009 | FRED COUPLES was between clubs but kept his cool—typical for the unflappable bopper called Boom-Boom. | *Photograph by* ROBERT BECK

2009 | 'X' MARKED the spot where clubs crossed as Tiger Woods and caddie Steve Williams saved steps during a practice round. | *Photograph by* ROBERT BECK

1970 - 1982

The Polyester Era

THE ERA'S BEST

Jack Nicklaus

From the day he turned pro in 1961 through 1980, the Golden Bear finished in the top 10 in 240 of the 367 official events he played in, taking home the trophy 70 times.

Gary Player

The "Black Knight" from South Africa logged more than 14 million air miles while winning tournaments on six continents. During the 1970s he won 44 times in eight countries.

Tom Watson

He outlasted Nicklaus in some of the game's most thrilling duels, and collected five claret jugs, two green jackets and a U.S. Open championship between 1975 and '83.

Lee Trevino

A Masters title escaped him, but the fan favorite won the other three majors twice apiece, though he captured only one major title after being struck by lightning in 1975.

Kathy Whitworth

Averaging 3.8 victories a year over a 23-year span, the Texan won an LPGA-record 88 tournaments and in 1981 became the first woman to top $1 million in career earnings.

>MILESTONES<

1972
JUSTIN LEONARD
Born June 15

1974
PLAYERS CHAMPIONSHIP
Held for the first time

1975
LEE ELDER
Breaks Masters color barrier

1975
ELDRICK "TIGER" WOODS
Born December 30

1976
WOMEN'S BRITISH OPEN
Debuts at Fulford Golf Club

1978
THE LEGENDS OF GOLF
Senior tour's precursor born

1979
RYDER CUP
Now open to all European players

1980
SERGIO GARCÍA
Born January 9

1980
U.S. SENIOR OPEN
Played for the first time

1982
KATHY WHITWORTH >
Breaks LPGA wins record

NOW OPEN FOR PLAY

TPC Sawgrass (Stadium)
PONTE VEDRA BEACH, FLORIDA
1981 / Designed by Pete Dye

< GOLFERS LOSE MORE THAN 100,000 BALLS A YEAR IN THE POND THAT RINGS THE FAMED ISLAND-GREEN 17TH.

Muirfield Village
DUBLIN, OHIO
1974 / Jack Nicklaus & Desmond Muirhead

Valderrama
SOTOGRANDE, SPAIN
1974 / Robert Trent Jones

Castle Pines
CASTLE ROCK, COLORADO
1981 / Jack Nicklaus

>> GOLF IN THE REAL WORLD <<

Moon Shots February 6, 1971 Alan Shepard, commander of Apollo 14, > carries a scoop with the head of a six-iron attached to it onto the lunar surface and takes a pair of one-handed swings, shanking the first ball, then smacking the other "miles and miles and miles" (with help from lunar gravity one-sixth that of Earth's). No one knows what happened to either ball.

Dead Solid Perfect 1971 Written by SI's Dan Jenkins, the game's most popular comic novel pokes ribald fun at life on the PGA Tour and inspires an underrated '88 TV movie starring Randy Quaid as journeyman pro Kenny Lee Puckett.

The Open Opens Up June 18 and 19, 1977 Viewers get to watch the final two rounds of the U.S. Open in their entirety as ABC Sports broadcasts all 36 holes of weekend action live from Southern Hills. An estimated seven million viewers see Hubert Green edge Lou Graham for the trophy.

Telegenic Tiger Cub October 6, 1978 Two-year old Tiger Woods dazzles Bob Hope, Jimmy Stewart and a studio audience on TV's *Mike Douglas Show*, driving balls into a screen with near-perfect form and rolling putts with Hope while proud papa Earl looks on.

Hi Noonan July 25, 1980 The quintessential golf comedy premieres. Co-written by Douglas Kenney, Brian Doyle-Murray and Harold Ramis and starring Bill Murray—the last three former caddies—*Caddyshack* remains one of the most-quoted movies ever. The noises made by Mr. Gopher are recorded dolphin sounds.

Ringing Endorsement 1982 Sales of Uniden's cordless telephones skyrocket after Jack Nicklaus plugs them in TV commercials. Nicklaus becomes one of advertising's top pitchmen, representing American Express, Magic Chef, Manville and Pontiac.

Four golfers playing for money were hunting for a ball in deep rough. One said, "Here's my ball!" Another cried, "He's a liar. I've got his ball in my pocket!"

BEST SHOT

JULY 15, 1972

Lee Trevino

Following three poor shots on the par-5 17th at Muirfield, with Jack Nicklaus one stroke behind, Trevino chips out of the rough. The ball falls in for a birdie, and the ebullient Trevino holds on for his second straight British Open title.

WORST SHOT

JULY 11, 1970

Doug Sanders

Facing a three-footer to win the British Open and avenge a second-place Open finish to Jack Nicklaus in '66, Sanders pushes his putt, leading to an 18-hole playoff with Nicklaus the next day, which Sanders loses by a stroke.

> THE SWING *Golden Bear* JACK NICKLAUS *may have had a flying right elbow but he got to a classic "reverse c" finish.*

> GOLF EVOLVES

GRAPHITE SHAFTS These lightweight alternatives to steel appear in 1973 and gain popularity during the '80s as golfers learn to love the increased swing speed they can deliver. By the '90s graphite dominates the driver- and fairway-wood markets.

UTILITY CLUBS The first trouble club to hit golf shops is the Cobra Baffler, a 25° utility metal introduced in 1975. The Baffler helps weekend golfers hit long, high shots from tricky lies; its successors will make long irons practically obsolete.

LAUNCH LIMITS In 1976 the USGA sets its Overall Distance Standard, banning balls that tend to go more than 280 yards when struck by a robot nicknamed "Iron Byron" in honor of sweet-swinging Byron Nelson.

OUT OF THE FRYING PAN Wet feet plague fewer golfers after 1976, when Bob Gore develops Gore-Tex, a porous form of polytetrafluoroethylene, a.k.a. Teflon.

GAME CHANGER: STIMPMETER
Invented by Massachusetts Amateur champion Eddie Stimpson in 1935 and first used at the '77 U.S. Open, the simple yardsticklike device provides consistent measurements of putting-surface speed.

>> FROM THE VAULT

"A SHORT PAR-3, *like death or a banana peel, is a great equalizer. Those little 110-to 150-yarders are the only holes where the duffer can hope to match the club champion or even a professional. Put simply, if I ever had to go head to head with a 100-shooter on one given hole, I wouldn't choose a short par-3. Give me a long par-5, enough room for the duffer to make some mistakes.*" —JACK NICKLAUS *in* SI, MAY 20, 1974

> ON THE NUMBER

71 Gene Sarazen's age when he aced the "Postage Stamp" 8th hole at Royal Troon during the 1973 British Open. A day later he sank a sand shot for birdie at the same hole.

67 Sam Snead's age when he made the cut at the 1979 Westchester Classic, becoming the oldest golfer to advance to the weekend at a PGA Tour event.

3 Claret jugs won by Jack Nicklaus, whose British Open triumph at St. Andrews in 1978 made him the first player to capture each of the four majors at least three times.

17 Consecutive seasons Kathy Whitworth had at least one LPGA victory, starting in 1962.

2 Strokes Robert Impaglia was penalized for slow play at the 1978 U.S. Open, the first slow-play penalty in tournament history.

10 Consecutive Ryder Cup victories for the United States—leading to the expansion of Great Britain & Ireland's team to add players from all of Europe in 1979.

3 Consecutive NCAA individual titles, starting in 1971, for University of Texas golfer Ben Crenshaw, the first and only player in college history to three-peat.

2004 | LE TOUESSROK Golf Course is the only game in town on Île aux Cerfs, off Africa's eastern coast in the Indian Ocean. | *Photograph by* DAVID CANNON

1999 | THE PACE of play was glacial at the World Ice Golf Championships, but the scenery sent chills up golfers' spines. | *Photograph by* SIMON BRUTY

CHOOSE YOUR WEAPON

BY E.M. SWIFT

Almost 20 years ago the author wondered whether high-tech equipment would revolutionize the game. —*from* SI, JULY 9, 1990

YOU BEGIN TO GET THE IDEA that maybe golf manufacturers are out of control when you find out that they are making clubs and balls out of components used in nuclear weapons and bulletproof vests. I mean, progress is great and all, but when a sleeve of golf balls sets off the alarm at airport security, and when alloys once used in the struts of a Gemini space capsule show up in your irons, you wonder whether we're on the right track. What we are talking about here is a game.

A game whose increasingly sophisticated tools are compromising, in the opinion of many, the time-honored elements of skill, practice and judgment. Want to hit the ball far? May we suggest an aerodynamically designed graphite-headed driver from Yonex, the A.D.X. 200. The half-grapefruit-sized clubhead, with a sweet spot 20% larger than normal, is oversize but lightweight, and it is attached to a 45-inch graphite/boron shaft that is two inches longer than standard. Increased club length translates, by the oxymoron of simple physics, into increased clubhead speed; ergo, greater distance. You'll drive the ball, the company estimates, an average of 11.7% farther than usual.

Or perhaps you would prefer something in cobalt chromium, a metal so hard it is used to make artificial hips. Combined with a graphite shaft, a cobalt chromium clubhead will add 10 yards to your drives or your money back. The Lynx company guarantees it.

Are synthetic polymers more your style? Cobra recently came out with the Ultramid, a driver made of a high-tech thermoplastic originally developed by scientists for use in bulletproof vests. Whichever set of clubs you prefer, you will want a golf ball that explodes off the club face. Something in lithium, perhaps, the metal of choice of nine out of 10 nuclear physicists who have designed a hydrogen bomb. Talk about getting more bang for your buck. Just don't let the Iraqis get their hands on the Ram Tour Lithium Plus.

Windy day? Want to hit it low? Forget choking down and pretending you're Lee Trevino. It's simpler to run out and buy a three-pack of Titleist's 384 Low Trajectory balatas, whose icosahedron-patterned dimples have been designed to cheat the wind, not to mention the club pro who teaches good shot making.

The fact is, for almost any difficulty in golf, there is a high-tech remedy for sale that was not on the market 10 years ago. Got the yips? Buy a long putter, the pendulum-like contraption that uses the player's sternum to anchor the top hand. This is a golf swing?

Got a slice? Perennial banana-bonkers can now whale away with abandon, knowing that metal woods used in conjunction with two-piece, Surlyn-covered balls will absolutely, positively impart less spin on impact than their old persimmons did.

The sweet spot of a golf club, once the size of a dime—the exact location of which, worn smooth, can be found on Ben Hogan's one-iron, on display in Golf House, the United States Golf Association museum in Far Hills, N.J.—is now the size of an Oreo cookie. Shots that once squirted off the toe of a six-iron now fly straight and true toward the green, thanks to the miracle of perimeter weighting. And who knows what lies ahead as golf manufacturers race to harness the powers of Kevlar and ceramics and compounds unknown?

Where will it all end? And who, pray tell, has been minding the store while the club and ball manufacturers have busied themselves with all manner of schemes—some bogus, some legitimate—to diminish the skill factors in golf, making it increasingly difficult to distinguish the great golfers from the nearly great, and the good golfers from the pretty good? Is the game becoming too easy?

"Easier, yes. Too easy? No," says Don Callahan, head pro at The Country Club, in Brookline, Mass., which was host to the 1988 U.S. Open. "The ball is livelier and the clubheads more forgiving, which is making the game more fun for the average golfer. But instead of hitting a dozen good shots a round, he's probably hitting 18."

Wally Uihlein, president and CEO of Titleist, echoes those sentiments. "I talk to very few amateurs who say, 'Wally, I'm playing too good. Let's make the game harder.' I know that my handicap isn't the lowest it's ever been. Is yours?"

As a matter of fact, no. And according to the USGA, which historically has safeguarded the best interests of the game, neither is the average golfer's. The median handicap for men today is 17, the same as it was 25 years ago. . . .

THE OLD balata balls, rubber-coated bundles of rubber bands, have given way to two-, three- and four-piece polyurethane missiles that fly farther and straighter.

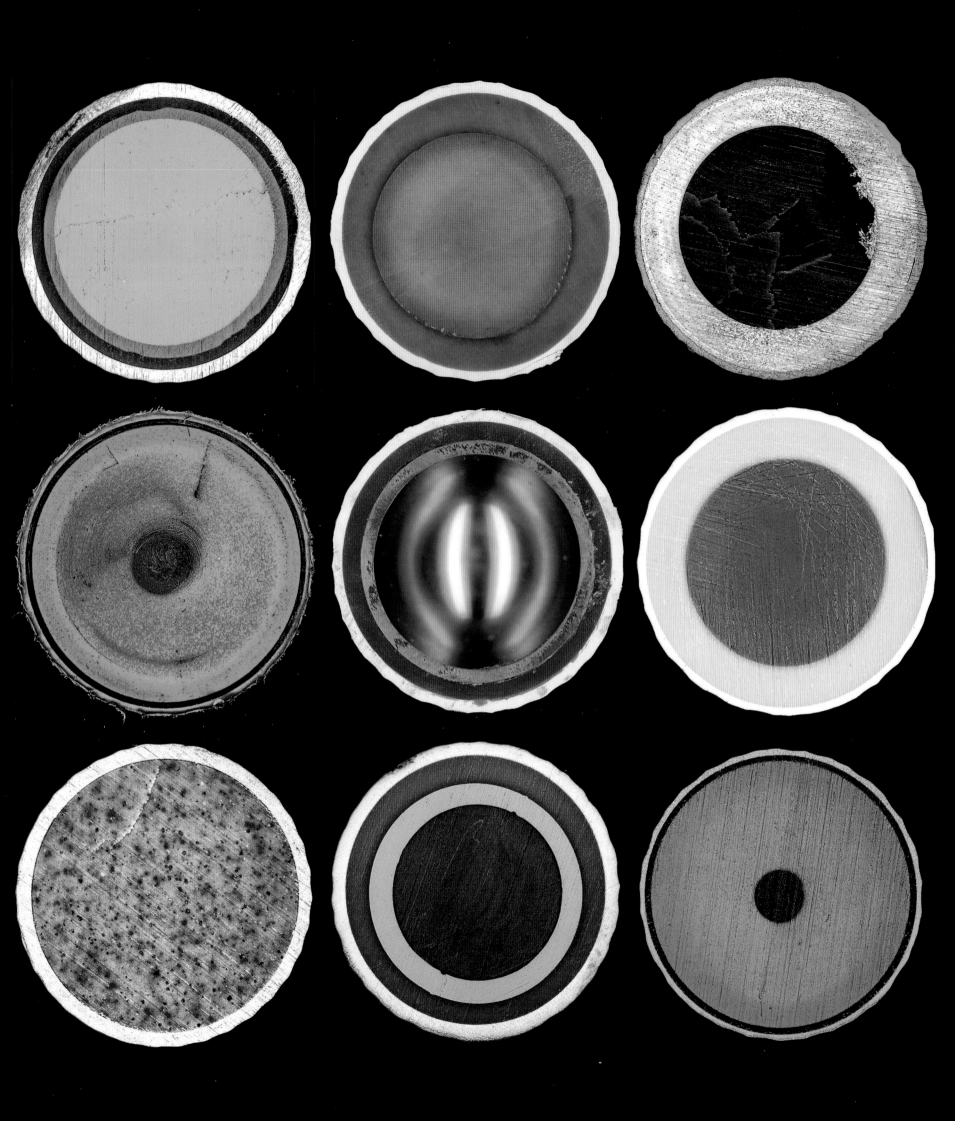

2002 | UNEASY AT the Ryder Cup, Phil Mickelson punched his way out and helped partner David Toms notch a point for the U.S. team. | *Photograph by* FRED VUICH

2007 | SNAP-HOOKING his four-iron at the Masters, Tiger Woods sacrificed the club and finished two shots behind Zach Johnson. | *Photograph by* ROBERT BECK

1960 | PERHAPS THE least-heralded golf great, Billy Casper won three majors and 48 other titles while lining up against Nicklaus and Palmer. | *Photograph by* JERRY COOKE

1930 | OLYMPIC DIVING gold medalist Helen Meany took up golf at the Greenbrier Resort and was briefly back in her element. | *Photograph by* USGA MUSEUM

THE DAY FRANCIS NEARLY FELL

BY BERNARD DARWIN

Almost half a century after acting as Francis Ouimet's scorekeeper during the 1913 U.S. Open—and signing the scorecard below— English golf writer Darwin, the evolutionist's grandson, looked back on a tournament that changed the game.

—*from* SI, SEPTEMBER 3, 1956

EVERY GAME HAS ITS INTENSE moments which fix themselves forever in the memory. To the swifter moving games belong those instants of victory or defeat which pass almost as the speed of thought. The historic moments of golf are slower and more drawn-out and, for that very reason, perhaps the harder to bear. The hush that falls upon a golfing crowd as the player studies a fateful putt is full of agony. I have many visions from Scottish links of a big, black square of people watching and waiting around the green with only the cry of curlews overhead to break that eerie silence.

These moments are apt to be capricious. While some have been obviously filled with impending doom, others have been apparently trifling accompaniments to the big show, and yet it is they that remain when the rest have faded. It is now 70 years since golf and I were first acquainted, and I will try to pick out of memory's storehouse a few instants of golfing time which are to me unforgettable.

The account of Francis Ouimet's triumph over Harry Vardon and Ted Ray has been written many times. The rain, the sodden ground, the puddles on the polo field, the damp, raw fog hanging above the treetops, the towels to keep the clubs dry, the crowds pouring out from Boston to see the heroic young defender of his country, the blare of the megaphones—they are still fresh in memory after three-and-forty years; but one moment stands out among the many, not from the playing off of the tie but from Francis's great spurt on the day before which made a tie of it. Several others had had their chances of catching the two Englishmen; one by one they had fallen down; only Francis had held on, and he had nearly fallen. Now there are only two holes left to play, two good stiff par-4 holes, and he has got to do them in seven strokes to tie. At the 17th he plays a beautiful second but is still left with a curly downhill putt. How long? I do not now trust myself to say, but will hazard 15 feet. The ball takes the curve to perfection, and in it miraculously goes. And then comes the unforgettable scene. I look at the people round me, substantial citizens of Boston, and they all seem to have gone suddenly mad. Their mouths are wide-open, their eyes jumping out of their heads, their hats waving in the air. And if ever people had the right, nay the duty to shout, they have it now.

Much the same scene is enacted at the same green next day when Francis holes the very same downhill putt for another 3. But the madness cannot be quite so glorious again. The first time it had come from the joy of being unbelievably saved; this time it is only the confirmation of certain salvation. Nothing can stop Francis now, and yet it is a comfort to see his ball soaring over the sodden cross-bunker to the haven where it would be. I suppose I signed the winner's card and handed it over to the constituted authorities, because I have seen it since at The Country Club, but I must have done so in a state of semiconsciousness.

Now we must have something of the immortal Bobby. A kind friend once said that he read anything I wrote on golf except about Bobby Jones; as to him there was nothing to say and superlatives were a bore. . . .

MOMENTS AFTER celebrating with fans and his 10-year-old caddie, Ouimet (held aloft) leaned toward a woman behind him and said, "Mother, I'll be home soon."

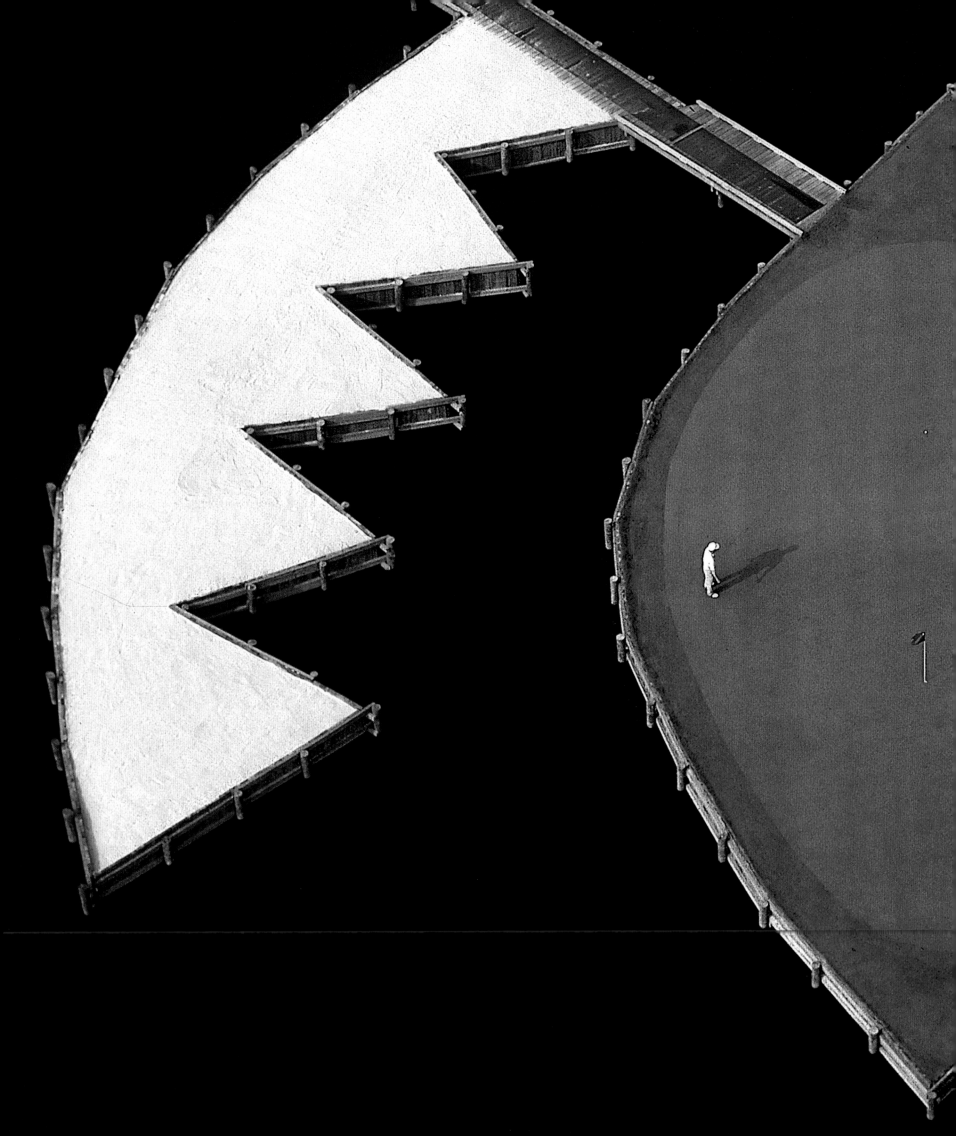

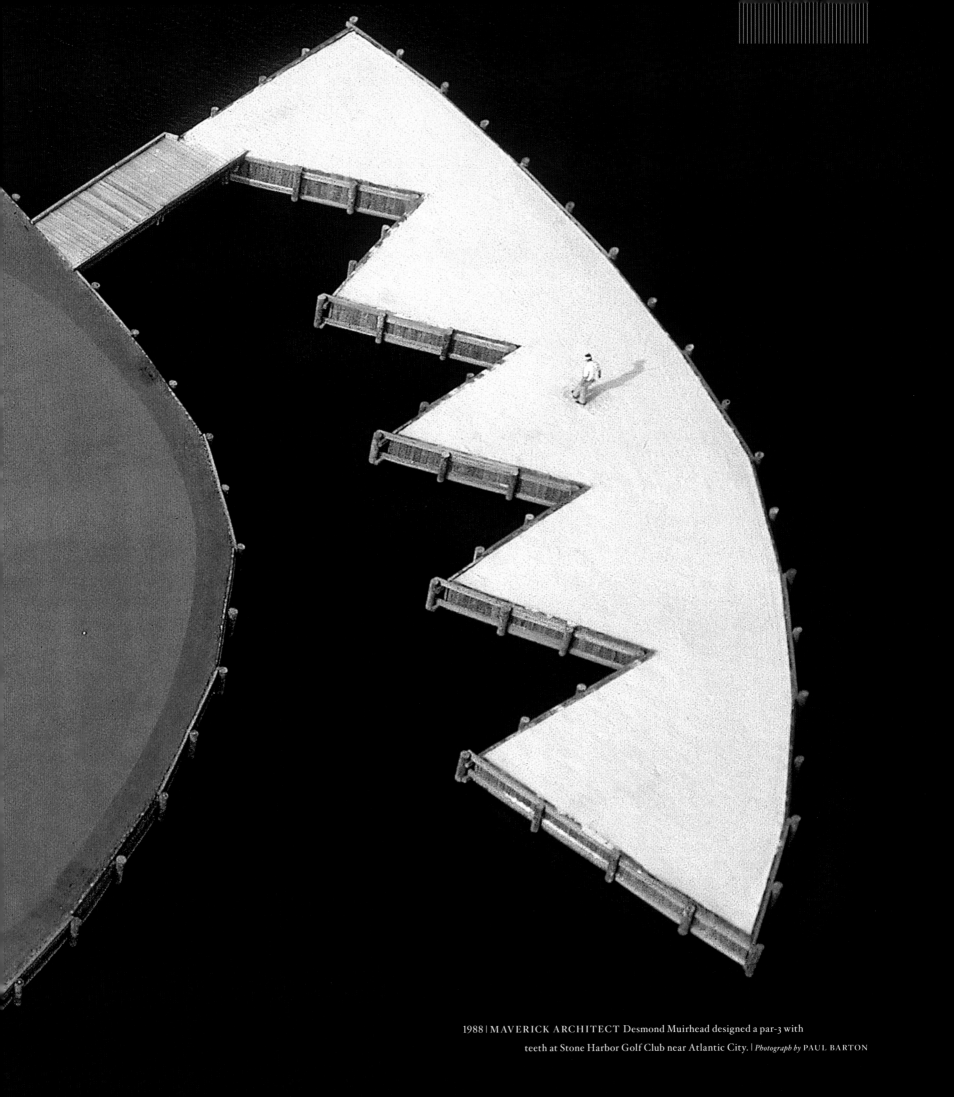

1988 | MAVERICK ARCHITECT Desmond Muirhead designed a par-3 with teeth at Stone Harbor Golf Club near Atlantic City. | *Photograph by* PAUL BARTON

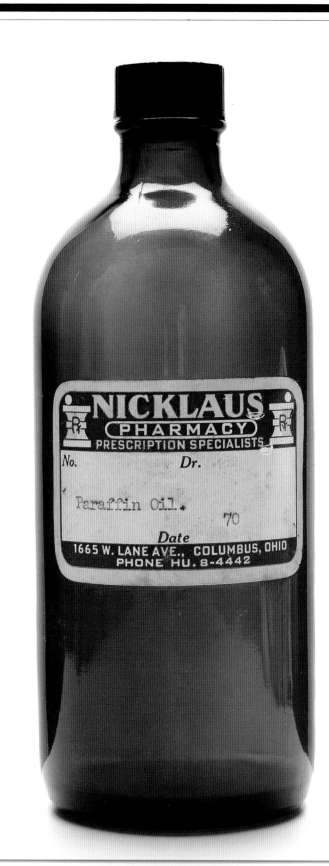

> **Prescriptions**

They Had the Cure

What did an Ohio pharmacist have in common with the Texas teaching pro who mentored Ben Crenshaw and Tom Kite? Both Charlie Nicklaus and Harvey Penick knew how to nurture young talent

1959 | CHARLIE'S PHARMACY

RELIEF FOR IRREGULAR CUSTOMERS   1960 | LIKE FATHER, LIKE SON

A BIG BLACK briefcase held the notes Penick boiled down into his best-selling *Little Red Book*; the last word in his shanks note is "pulling."

A NEW TWIST

BY ALAN SHIPNUCK

Teenager Sergio García made a memorable runner-up at Medinah, while the victor took a giant step forward. —from SI, AUGUST 23, 1999

THERE WAS NO FREIGHTED embrace with the old man behind the 18th green. There were no ghosts exorcised, no historical legacies razed. This was golf, not sociology. If Tiger Woods's stunning victory at the 1997 Masters signaled the birth of a cross-cultural icon, his win at last week's PGA Championship served mainly to confirm that he has matured into a golfer for the ages. For 3½ rounds Woods overpowered the longest course in major championship history, and then, in a giddy, sloppy, riveting duel over the final nine holes, he outlasted Spain's teen dream, Sergio García, who didn't quite sneak off with the tournament—but for a while did steal the show.

Woods's one-stroke victory, with an 11-under 277, put an exclamation point on a century of golf and launched a rivalry that should propel the game into a new era. Forget Nicklaus and Palmer; Woods, 23, and García, 19, have the star quality of Newman and Redford. What was the most electric moment of Sunday's back nine, anyway? Was it the mischievous glare García gave Woods after making a long birdie putt at the par-3 13th, which announced the beginning of El Niño's comeback? "It wasn't—I don't know how to say—it wasn't a bad thing," García said afterward in his courtly English. "I mean, I did it with good feelings, not hoping he would make a triple bogey or whatever. I was kind of telling him: If you want to win, you have to play well."

Perhaps what we will remember most about this sun-toasted afternoon at Medinah (Ill.) Country Club was García's recovery—and reveling—at the par-4 16th. Having cut the deficit to one, but with his drive cozied up to the base of one of Medinah's 4,161 trees (yes, someone counted), García opened the face of his six-iron and, with his eyes closed, slashed at the ball like a housewife trying to kill a mouse with a broom. He chased the shot up the fairway with hilarious enthusiasm, doing a little scissors kick as he strained to see it reach the green, and then pantomimed to the crowd the pitter-patter of his heart. Summing up Sunday's events, García said, "It was really fun, most of all. It was joy, it was pressure, it was, I will tell you, the best day of my life."

It also was a day that concluded with Woods kissing the Wanamaker Trophy, and that, in the end, is what the 81st PGA deserves to be remembered for. As a kid, Woods had a chronology of Jack Nicklaus's record 18 major championship victories tacked to the wall next to his bed, so he knows as well as anybody that by the end of Nicklaus's third full season as a pro he already had won three majors. Woods is still one down, but once again the race is on.

The long-awaited second leg of Woods's career Grand Slam was achieved with the kind of resolve that was Nicklaus's trademark. Tied for the lead and two shots in front of García as the final round began, Woods came out with four birdies in his first 11 holes, forging a seemingly insurmountable five-stroke lead. One three-putt, two gouged chips and a loose eight-iron later, he had spent four of those shots, and when he arrived at Medinah's 17th hole, he was facing one of the defining moments of his young career. It didn't help that for the first time his antagonist was younger than he was and the crowd was rooting against him. "I knew when I got to 17 I had to play the two best holes of my life," said Woods after his victory. "Despite everything that had happened, I still had the lead, and I was completely focused on doing whatever I had to do to maintain it."

The 17th hole at Medinah is a steeply downhill par-3 over water that was playing 212 yards on Sunday, and Woods misjudged both the swirling winds and his adrenaline. He jacked a six-iron over the green and into a gnarly clump of Kentucky bluegrass. Legs splayed in an awkward stance, he fluffed the ensuing chip, leaving himself a frightening downhill eight-footer for par. It was the kind of putt on which a reputation can turn, but Woods willed his ball into the left corner of the cup, and that was the key shot of the tournament. . . .

AFTER TIGER WOODS applied body English to a recovery shot (above), an even-younger star celebrated a miracle shot with some jubilant body Spanish.

1999 | THE TOP player on earth, David Duval, got his mind off golf and Tiger Woods, who would soon pass him in the World Ranking. | *Photograph by* GREGORY HEISLER

1930s | LIKE PLENTY of duffers wielding drivers, W.C. Fields spent his day grumbling about the one that got away. | *Photograph by* MOVIE STILL ARCHIVES

> **Fifties Fashion**

Haberdashing Heroes

SI's preview of the 1955 U.S. Open featured six contenders, including 25-year-old Arnold Palmer,
"giving dramatic proof that golfers are maintaining their reputation as the best-dressed men in sport."

ARNOLD PALMER

PETER THOMSON

JULIUS BOROS

TOMMY BOLT

GENE LITTLER

BUD HOLSCHER

1954 | PLAYERS LEFT their bags in a clump on Sunday morning at the Masters, the day before Sam Snead edged Ben Hogan in a playoff. | *Photograph by* MARK KAUFFMAN

RICHARD MEEK (6)

2009 | GARY PLAYER bowed to tradition at the close of the Masters, an event he won three times and played in for 52 years in a row. | *Photograph by* DON EMMERT

1968 | THE GOOD GUY wore black at Carnoustie, which British Open champ Player called "the hardest course there is." | *Photograph by* GERRY CRANHAM

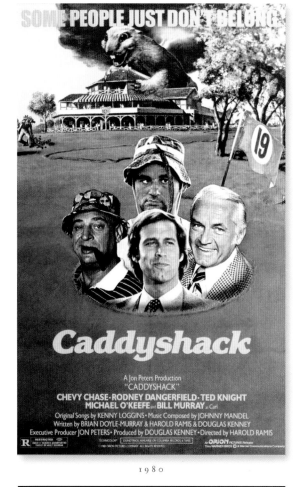

1980

> Golf in Reel Life

Fairways and Screens

*Filmmakers have churned out golf movies since the 1896 silent short
'Golfing Extraordinary,' with comedies dominating the field—perhaps
because the game itself provides enough drama for most players*

1934   2007   1930

2000

1938

1996

1926

1953

1944

1996

WHEN THE NEWS ARRIVED

BY JIM MURRAY

This report from the 1955 U.S. Open, in which Jack Fleck forced a playoff with Ben Hogan, ran as an unsigned sidebar to Herbert Warren Wind's main story. Turns out it was by a stringer, James Murray, who as "Jim" went on to be a Hall of Fame sportswriter. —*from* SI, JUNE 27, 1955

IN THE LOCKER ROOM, BEN HOGAN sank heavily on a bench and took a Scotch and water from somebody's hand. It seemed certain that his 287 had clinched his fifth championship. He sipped his drink, shook his head and said slowly: "Boys, if I win it, I'll never work at this again. It's just too tough getting ready for a tournament. This one doggone near killed me. Besides, I don't think it's fair to drag Valerie [Mrs. Hogan] around and put her through this every time." Someone asked if his leg had bothered him. "Only my knee," said Ben. "The more I walked, the more it hurt."

From the end of the row of lockers an attendant shouted: "Jack Fleck is on 16 and he needs one birdie on the last three to tie!" Hogan sipped his drink, then smiled thinly: "Good for him." A reporter asked: "Which hole do you think you won it on, Ben?" He frowned: "There's no one hole. You don't win tournaments on just one hole. There's 72 holes."

A newcomer burst into the group. "Fleck's parred 17!" he cried. "Just missed his birdie. Needs a birdie on 18 to tie." Hogan stood up. He stepped out of his slacks, revealing a bandaged left knee. "I got to take a shower," he said. He walked off, stiff-legged. There was small talk, then the group was silent until Ben returned. He pulled on his slacks, slipped on his tasseled shoes, grinned as he looked around.

Another runner arrived, panting. "Fleck's in the rough on the 18th," he shouted. Everyone turned back to Hogan. He reached into his locker, pulled out his tie and slowly began

knotting it. Incredibly, somebody decided to ask: "Ben, did you use your own clubs, the ones you manufacture, in the tournament?" Hogan whirled and exploded: "Of course I did! Are you kidding?" Jack Burke walked in, began to wrestle with his locker. "What did you do, boy?" Hogan called to him. "No good, Ben," Burke answered. "Drove in the rough all day." Tommy Bolt came in, elaborately avoided Topic A: "Hey, Benny, you got me all fouled up down there at Fort Worth. You got me to fix that hook. Now, doggone it, I'm slicing the ball. I'm goin' back to hookin'. You son of a gun, I bet you did that a-purpose." Hogan smiled. Cary Middlecoff appeared, stuck out his hand. "Wonderful tournament, Ben, wonderful," he said. "A damn good score." He hurried away. Hogan drew on his jacket, reached into his locker and took out his clubs and threw them on the floor. "Anybody want a club cover?" he asked affably. Before anyone could answer, a new informant rushed in. "Ben, Fleck's got an eight-foot putt to tie!"

Hogan relaxed. No one could think of anything to say for a moment. Then, desperately, a man brought up the subject of Ben's club manufacturing business again. "Now, how many clubs will you make in a day, Ben?" he asked. "It comes to 460 sets a month," Hogan said. "Isn't it true, Ben," the man rushed on, "that you threw away a hundred thousand clubs because they weren't perfect?" Hogan nodded. "I got at least $150,000 worth of new clubs I won't ship." He sat down on the bench again. The group fell silent.

Then it came: a tremendous roar from the gallery at the 18th. A reporter whispered hoarsely: "The kid's sunk it!" Ben Hogan's head went down and he cursed softly. Then he lifted his head and looked around at them all. "I was wishing he'd either make a two or a five," he said. "I was wishing it was over—all over." He turned to an attendant, indicated his clubs and sighed. "Well, we might as well git those things back in the locker. Gotta play tomorrow, looks like." . . .

AFTER WAITING OUT Fleck's fourth-round finish, Hogan lost the next day's playoff and congratulated the underdog winner.

1991 | LEFTY WADKINS, better known as Lanny, did an about-face with his putter at the War by the Shore Ryder Cup. | *Photograph by* JACQUELINE DUVOISIN

2003 | TROUBLED TOM KITE chopped his way to an unsightly double bogey in the Senior British Open at Turnberry. | *Photograph by* BOB MARTIN

2007 | A CLAW GRIP helped Chris DiMarco cure his putting woes and come within a lip-out of a 2005 Masters victory. | *Photograph by* DAVID CANNON

1993 | BERNHARD LANGER got a handle on his short game, overcame the yips and claimed his second green jacket. | *Photograph by* JOHN IACONO

1983 - 1995

A Growing Game

JOHN DALY
Power personified
1993
Photograph by JOHN BIEVER

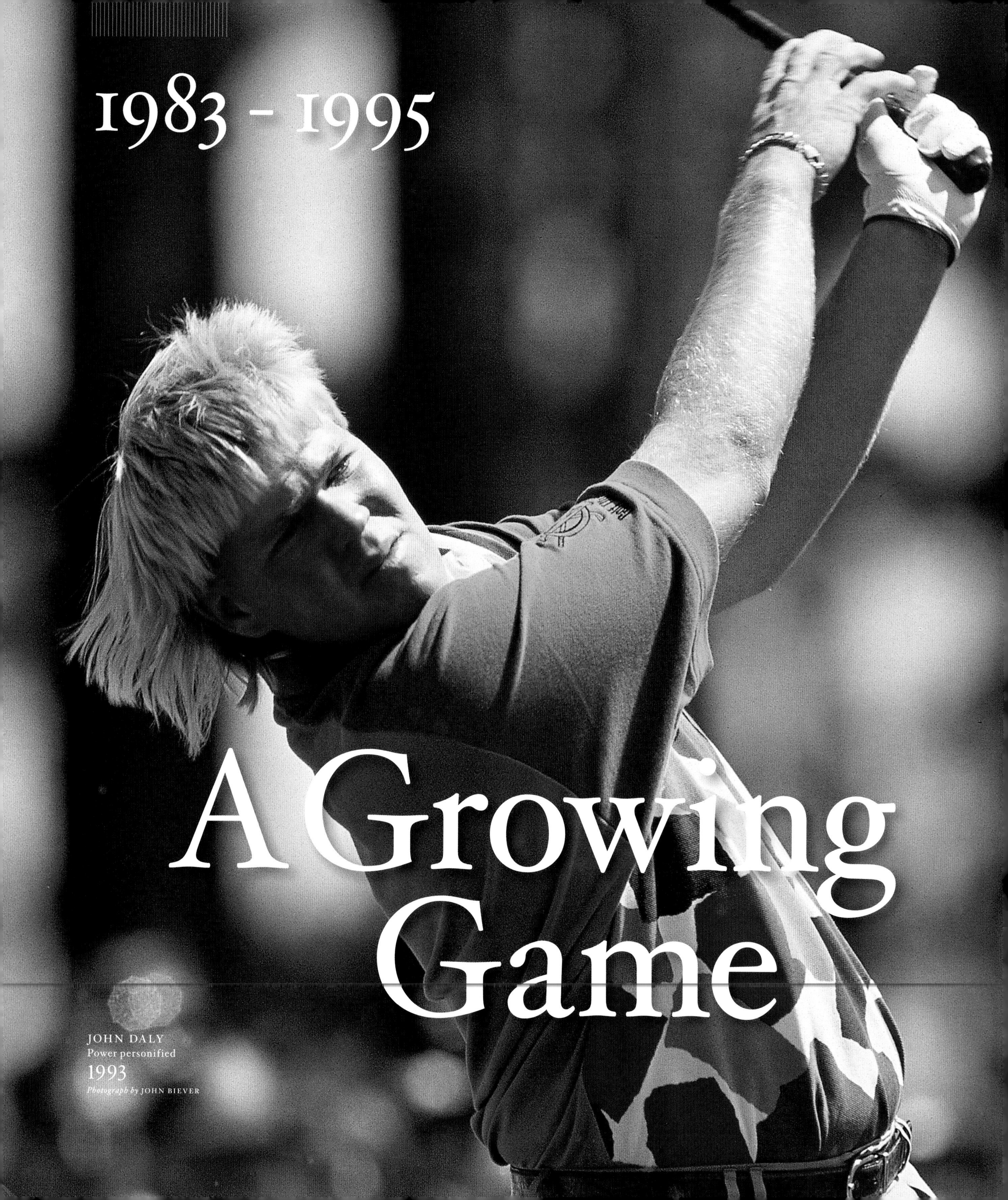

THE ERA'S BEST

Seve Ballesteros

The heart and soul of European golf won five majors in a 10-year span from 1979 to '88, spent 61 weeks as the world's No. 1 and brought matchless verve and passion to the game.

Nick Faldo

The former "Foldo" remade his swing and didn't finish outside the top 20 in a Grand Slam event from 1988 to '93. Four of his six major titles came by a single stroke or in a playoff.

Greg Norman

His shocking sinkings make it easy to forget the Great White Shark's two British Opens and 90 international wins; he was the world's top-ranked player for six years.

Nick Price

During the mid-'90s he won two PGA Championships and a British Open and went through a stretch in which he hoisted trophies in 16 of 54 events he entered.

Nancy Lopez

In 1985 the dominant female player of the late '70s made a triumphant comeback, reclaiming the LPGA money title with five victories and five runner-up finishes.

>MILESTONES<

1983
SKINS GAME
Debuts at Desert Highlands

1983
JIMMY DEMARET
Three-time Masters champ dies

1985
ANTHONY KIM
Born June 19

1989
MICHELLE WIE
Born October 11

1990
JACK NICKLAUS
Wins his Senior tour debut

1990
FIRST SOLHEIM CUP >
Lopez leads U.S. women

1992
TIGER WOODS
Plays his first PGA Tour event

1994
PRESIDENTS CUP
First U.S. vs. International match

1995
HARVEY PENICK
Teaching legend dies at 90

1995
WORLD CUP OF GOLF
Played at Mission Hills in China

NOW OPEN FOR PLAY

Sand Hills
MULLEN, NEBRASKA
1995 / Designed by Bill Coore & Ben Crenshaw
< COORE AND CRENSHAW THREADED STRIPS OF PRISTINE
GREEN THROUGH WINDSWEPT PRAIRIE.

Shadow Creek
NORTH LAS VEGAS, NEVADA
1989 / Tom Fazio & Steve Wynn

Kiawah Island (Ocean)
KIAWAH ISLAND, SOUTH CAROLINA
1991 / Pete Dye

Loch Lomond
LUSS, SCOTLAND
1994 / Tom Weiskopf & Jay Morrish

>> GOLF IN THE REAL WORLD <<

Dorf's Duffs 1987 The first *Dorf on Golf* tape hits video-store shelves. The faux-instructional farce stars TV comic Tim Conway as golf goof Derk Dorf, a diminutive hacker with a thick Swedish accent and a bag full of gadgets and tricks.

Golden Moment 1989 The original Golden Tee Golf arcade > game, from Incredible Technologies, features a zooming trackball and commentary by Peter Jacobsen. ("It's sand-o-rama time!") An estimated 10 million golfers will play more than a billion rounds as Golden Tee goes on to earn $3 billion for the game-maker and countless bar owners.

Red Makes Green 1992 *Harvey Penick's Little Red Book,* the collected wisdom of the 87-year-old golf guru from Austin, Texas, climbs the best-seller lists. Penick's tome becomes the top sports hardcover of all time, with more than 1 million copies sold.

TGC Teed Up February 10, 1993 Arnold Palmer and partner Joe Gibbs announce plans for The Golf Channel, which they promise will "make a wide variety of golf information, instruction and entertainment available to players and fans worldwide."

Thar She Tries to Blow February 10, 1994 The world's least convincing marine biologist, *Seinfeld*'s George Costanza saves a beached whale by pulling a golf ball (driven seaward by a wild-swinging Cosmo) from its blowhole. Kramer: "Is that a Titleist? A hole in one, huh?"

Snoopy the Flying Ace 1994 The precocious beagle in Charles M. Schulz's *Peanuts* comic strip debuts as the blimp-borne mascot of MetLife insurance. His flights on the MetLife blimps *Snoopy One, Two* and *Three,* floating above golf tournaments, consitute a comeback for the doghouse pilot who had daydreamed of leading a Tour event only to be told dogs weren't allowed on the course.

GOLFER 1 IS AWAY
HOLE #1
PAR 4
43 YRDS
STROKE 4
WIND 1 MPH
SAND WEDGE RANGE 20-50 YDS.
MOVE TRACKBALL BACK FOR BACK SWING

God sliced his drive toward a lake. Suddenly the lake froze, the ball bounced straight up and a lightning bolt knocked it into the hole. Saint Peter said, "Are you going to play golf, or screw around?"

BEST SHOT

AUGUST 10, 1986

Bob Tway

Tway arrived at the 72nd green of the PGA Championship tied with Greg Norman. While Norman studied a 25-foot putt he hoped would win him the title, Tway holed a bunker shot, stealing yet another major from the Shark.

WORST SHOT

JULY 16, 1983

Hale Irwin

On Day 3 of the British Open, Irwin nonchalanted a backhanded tap-in on the 14th green at Royal Birkdale—and whiffed it! History's biggest whiff came back to haunt Irwin, who finished one stroke behind winner Tom Watson.

> THE SWING   *Greg Norman got wide on the backswing, produced loads of lag and swung so hard his feet left the ground.*

> GOLF EVOLVES

STEEP SLOPES In 1981 the USGA introduces the Slope Rating to indicate the difficulty of a course for bogey golfers, allowing better handicap comparisons—and bets. Slopes range from 55 to 155; at a rugged 144 from the tips, Bethpage Black is still 10 shots "easier" than Nevada's Wolf Creek.

LESSONS ON VIDEO Why go to the range when you can hone your game at home? The first golf-instruction video, Jack Nicklaus' *Golf My Way*, hits VCRs in 1983.

SQUARE GROOVES After Ping sues the PGA Tour over its 1988 move to ban square grooves in irons, the Tour spends four years tied up in court before giving up.

SPIKES GO SOFT Developed in 1993 as part of an effort to limit the damage metal spikes inflict on greens during winter, turf-friendly plastic cleats would soon make the steel kind obsolete. No longer would golfers clack their way through parking lots.

GAME CHANGER: BIG BERTHA
Callaway wowed crowds at the 1991 PGA Merchandise Show by introducing the Big Bertha. With a 190-cc steel head, Bertha *(top)* paved the way for later models including today's 460-cc behemoths.

> ON THE NUMBER

14 Career playoff victories for Jack Nicklaus, tying Arnold Palmer for the most in Tour history. By outlasting Andy Bean at his own tournament, the Memorial, Nicklaus reached the milestone in 1984.

14 Consecutive years (1995–2008) in which Davis Love III earned at least $1 million, a Tour record. Tiger Woods was next with 13 and counting through '09.

26 Different winners in 37 LPGA events during the 1991 season, a tour record.

7 Wins in seven countries (England, France, Germany, Japan, Spain, Sweden and the U.S.) for Seve Ballesteros in 1988.

76 Qualifying-round score for Mary Bea Porter at the LPGA's 1988 Tucson Open. During her round the 38-year-old Porter scaled a fence beside the 13th hole to resuscitate a boy who had fallen into a swimming pool. The boy survived, and Porter was granted a special exemption into the tournament.

3 Consecutive U.S. Junior Amateur championships won by Tiger Woods from 1991 to '93. In the 60-year history of the nation's premier tournament for teenagers, no other player has ever won twice.

>> FROM THE VAULT

"HALE IRWIN, A THREE-TIME *U.S. Open champion, practically handed the Ryder Cup back to Europe by losing a 1-up lead over Langer with two holes to play in Sunday's final singles match. Irwin three-putted the 17th green and then fluffed a greenside pitch on number 18 for another bogey. 'I couldn't breathe, I couldn't swallow,' he said. 'The sphincter factor was high.'"*   —JOHN GARRITY *in* SI, OCTOBER 7, 1991

2009 | MUDDY DUDS weren't an option for Henrik Stenson, who stripped down at Doral to save his outfit, but couldn't save par; he made bogey. | *Photograph by* KYLE AUCLAIR

1890s | A ROYAL FOURSOME led by Queen Victoria's grandson Prince Albert (left) relaxed at Richmond Golf Club near London. | *Photograph by* BROWN BROTHERS

FOR YOU, HARVEY

BY RICK REILLY

Ben Crenshaw's Masters victory was an emotional tribute to the man who taught him the game. —from SI, APRIL 17, 1995

SO HOW WOULD *YOU* EXPLAIN IT? Balls trickling left down ridges, when any physicist would turn purple telling you they've got to go right. Putts diving into corners of holes when you know they are supposed to slide six feet past on green Formica. A ball on Saturday that had a one-way ticket for a double-bogey bunker at number 8, smacking dead into the sand and then, for no reason at all, bounding out.

"Another Harvey bounce," Julie Crenshaw would say to her husband, Ben, that night. Ben would smile yes.

And what about the caddie? What are the odds on *that?* Ben Crenshaw had come to Augusta for the Masters playing uglier than a presidential threesome. Three missed cuts in his last four starts. Hadn't broken 70 in two months. Sixty-ninth on the PGA Tour in putting. Sixty-ninth? Ben Crenshaw? But then on the Tuesday before the tournament, his longtime Augusta caddie, Carl Jackson, a man who would need two woofer implants just to be considered quiet, said out of the blue, "Put the ball a little bit back in your stance, Ben. And you got to turn your shoulders more."

After hitting four balls, Crenshaw was suddenly striping it again. Four balls! "I've never had a confidence transformation like that in my life," said Crenshaw.

The caddie?

Good thing, too, because for the 1984 Masters champion, practice was over. The next morning at 7:30 Crenshaw flew 950 miles to attend the funeral of Harvey Penick, the tiny and frail former head pro of Austin Country Club. In a downpour. Pure sentiment, but Crenshaw is 99.4% sentiment. This is a guy who watches *Beauty and the Beast* with his daughters and ends up crying himself. His father, Charlie, is also like that. Charlie will cry at a Thanksgiving toast or a decent Southwestern Bell ad. So three days after the 90-year-old Penick, the man who first put a golf club in Crenshaw's six-year-old hands and the only coach he ever had, died on Sunday, April 2, Crenshaw and Tom Kite, another of Penick's pupils from Austin, flew home and carried a very light box and their own heavy hearts to the grave.

After the service Penick's son, Tinsley, took his father's old wooden Gene Sarazen putter and saved it for Crenshaw. It was the same putter that, on the last Sunday in March, Penick, lying in a hospital bed in his bedroom at home, had commanded Crenshaw to get from the garage. The man who wrote *The Little Red Book* checked Crenshaw's grip the same way he had been checking it since Ben was a child. Then he said, "Just trust yourself."

When Crenshaw flew back to Augusta on Wednesday night he was tired and drained of tears and emotion and energy. But when he teed off in the tournament the next morning, all heaven broke loose. "There was this calmness to him all week that I have never seen before," said Julie.

Said Ben, "It was kind of like I felt this hand on my shoulder, guiding me along."

Crenshaw has always been a "feel" player, not only because of his hands but also because of his emotions. When things are going badly, he bleeds—he kicked a trash can a few years ago after a three-putt and may need surgery on that foot sometime soon—and his game unravels. However, when things start going well, Crenshaw lets his heart follow. The swing gets sweet, and the best putting stroke in history starts pouring golf balls into holes like little white rivers.

Moreover, every break went his way. Disaster never got within a three-wood of him. He made only five bogeys and not one double bogey. On Sunday, tied for the lead, he hit a terrible drive on the par-5 2nd hole. The ball struck a tree and bounced into the fairway, pretty as you please. "Look, there's Harvey," Julie said to a friend. Crenshaw birdied the hole.

What's weird is that this did not start out as Crenshaw's week at all. The first two days of the tournament belonged to the 19-year-old dervish known as Tiger Woods, the U.S. Amateur champ playing in his first Masters. . . .

INSPIRED BY THOUGHTS of mentor Penick, whom he and Kite helped bury, Crenshaw capped a moving week with his second Masters triumph.

1999 | JUSTIN LEONARD just jarred a 45-footer to spur the U.S. to victory in the Ryder Cup, triggering a home-team outburst that left Europe's golfers steaming. | *Photograph by* BOB MARTIN

1966 | EVENTUAL CHAMPION Jack Nicklaus found his ball in boy-high rough when the British Open came to Muirfield. | *Photograph by* AP

1993 | EVER-SCRAMBLING Seve Ballesteros saved par from everywhere and helped keep Europe close in the Ryder Cup. | *Photograph by* LANE STEWART

HOME ON THE RANGE

BY JOHN GARRITY

While searching in vain for his swing, the author discovered a species of golfer that reminded him of himself.

—*from* SI, NOVEMBER 13, 2000

YOUR RANGE RAT IS A MAN with a past. He's Bogie—no pun intended—bent over a bottle of bourbon in the dark of Rick's Café. He's James Stewart in *Vertigo*, tailing a beautiful woman through the streets of San Francisco because she reminds him of a lost love. Your range rat can be charming, even debonair, but golf has made him cynical. Like Sean Connery in a Bond flick, he has wakened too many times with a dead blonde sharing his pillow.

I speak from experience. For more than a decade I have haunted driving ranges from Minneapolis to Miyazaki, searching for a lost golf swing. I have hit balls off carpet squares, vinyl strips and gravel. I have hit off moldy mats into a night rain and watched the ball vanish above the lights and reappear as a splash in black water. I have aimed at trees, tractors, trampolines, yardage signs, fire trucks, bull's-eyes, pinball pods, rainbows and rafts. I have watched low-compression pitch-and-putt balls swoop and dart like June bugs in the floodlights. I have hit balls from wire buckets, drawstring bags and plastic paint cans. I have pushed computer cards into slots and watched balls pop up from underground. I have picked the gleaming white fruit of those elegant ball pyramids at golf schools and resorts.

Being a range rat is an interesting life, but it changes a man. Some years ago I was hitting balls at 2 a.m. at the Randall's Island Golf Range in New York City, when the cry of a baby distracted me. Turning around, I discovered that a Korean family had taken over a nearby bench. The mother was juggling baby bottles and blankets. A preschool girl slept on her grandmother's lap. Between shots, the father—who looked like a middle manager for Samsung—turned to his family and spoke in Korean. The women shook their heads vigorously and used their hands to show that his club face was closed on the takeaway.

A man wearing a sweatshirt and a ball cap walked up with two wire buckets of balls and took the station to my immediate right. The new arrival and I practiced for a while in silence, until he accidentally kicked over one of the buckets, sending balls bouncing down the concrete sidewalk behind the tee line. "Stop!" he yelled at the runaway balls. He turned to me and said, "I can hit O.K. when I'm a little buzzed. How about you?"

He then told me the story of his life. He was 39, married and childless. He loaded trucks for a living and drank beer most nights at a lounge. He said he had been playing golf for two years and, oh, yeah, he hoped someday to play on the Senior tour. "I don't hit it as good as Nicklaus and those guys," he said unnecessarily, "but I used to hustle pool, so maybe I can hustle golf."

He had a 7 o'clock tee time, and that's why he had come to Randall's Island when the bar closed instead of going home. He said, "I could use a few hours sleep, but when my head hits the pillow, I'm gone." He coughed. "Watch this. I can make the ball suck back like Greg Norman." He made a short, choppy swing and hit an ugly knuckleball that flew about 100 yards and hopped down the range like a jackrabbit. He shook his head and said, "Sometimes that's a *hard* sonofabitch to hit."

That's why I say the driving-range life changes a man. You start as a kid, swinging so hard with a cut-down five-iron that you stagger off the mat. You celebrate adolescence by taking your girl to the range and showing her how to hold the club while smart guys yell "Fore!" from passing cars. Before you know it, you're a character in a campy poster, smacking balls at the towers of the Triborough Bridge in the wee hours with James Dean on the mat behind you and Marilyn Monroe just up the tee line hitting soft wedges to the 50-yard sign.

Your range rat is afraid of commitment. He's John Cusack in *High Fidelity*, tallying the women who have left him. He's Hugh Grant in *Four Weddings and a Funeral*. Your range rat loves driving ranges, but he knows it's dangerous to invest too much emotion in any particular range. The two formative ranges of my youth in Kansas City—Smiley Bell's and Sam Snead's—gave way decades ago to a television studio and tract housing, respectively. (Range balls, oddly enough, linger for years, transmigrating through the soil by a process understood only by geologists. When bulldozers plowed up Smiley Bell's in 1969, old golf balls were found to a depth of eight feet.)

In Ireland this July I found the Ennis Driving Range padlocked and shuttered. In downtown San Diego, in August, I spied the high nets of a range from the window of my harborside hotel. When I drove to the site, I found a closed range overrun with weeds and trash. . . .

RANGE WARRIORS smack more than 10 million balls a year at New York City's Chelsea Piers, hoping to catch at least one just right.

MANNY MILLAN

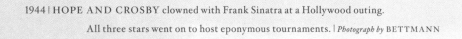

> Patrons of the Game

Hope and Glory

No celebrities did more to promote golf than Bing Crosby and Bob Hope. Crosby, a two handicap, was the better player, while hacker Hope employed a gag foot wedge, a self-aligning putter and a fellow named Nicklaus (right) to help with his line readings.

"HOPE FOOTWEDGE"

2001 | A TWILIGHT golfer at Australia's Anglesea Club may have rued the day he drew such an unruly gallery. | *Photograph by* BOB MARTIN

2006 | LATE-DAY SUN revealed every hill and swale at The Island Golf Club, 15 minutes from Dublin. | *Photograph by* ANTHONY EDGEWORTH

THE BABE WAKES UP

BY JOAN FLYNN DREYSPOOL

Babe Didrikson Zaharias, once the world's best female athlete, was nearing the end of a long battle with cancer when she and her husband, George, a former pro wrestler, invited the author to their Florida home. —from SI, MAY 14, 1956

"SH-SH-SH," GEORGE ZAHARIAS cautioned. "Babe is sleeping. Yesterday we went to St. Pete to the Ladies' PGA. Babe presented the prizes. When she walked up on the green, they all applauded for the longest time, the kind of applause that makes goose pimples—and Babe had 'em. "She wants to go everywhere," he added, "but she pays for it." His gaze strayed frequently to a black inter-communicating box in the kitchen wall of the Zahariases' modern redwood ranch house in Tampa. A similar black box was at his wife's bedside. When she awakened, she would call him.

A guest room and bath opened off the back of the kitchen, and to the side was a double garage with two Cadillacs in it. One of them had a sleeping bed fixed up in back for the Babe to stretch out on, since sitting for too long a time is painful for her.

In the thickly carpeted living room, softly lit shelves were filled with silver trophies of all shapes and sizes. Over the fireplace was a portrait of the Babe, painted in 1934.

The face was young, eager, intense. Her light brown hair was brushed back in a boyish bob and she was wearing a sleeveless jersey.

To the right of the mantel, in what appeared to be a place of honor, a glass-enclosed shadow box held a red satin, heart-shaped candy box cover, decked in ribbons and roses and set on black velvet. On it, in gold, were the words, "To My Wife on Valentine's Day."

In the right wing of the house, there were two bedrooms, baths and a den. The door to the master bedroom was closed. There was still no sound from it.

George Zaharias walked quietly, speaking low if at all.

A buzzing noise came over the intercom box. Zaharias went to it eagerly. "How you doin', honey?" he asked.

"Pretty good." The voice sounded far away and weak.

"Turn your box off," Zaharias teased, "we're talking about you."

"Spin off!" The old Didrikson spirit and verve were in her rejoinder.

Then the whole house came alive. Eddie, the Zaharias' 19-year-old helper, a bandana over the pincurls in her blonde hair, started brewing some hot liquid mixture, and Bebe, a frisky black miniature poodle which had been playing in the yard, scratched at the door to come in.

She went yapping at Zaharias's heels into the bedroom.

Moments later, the Babe's voice, brighter, stronger, came over the intercom. "Eddie, will you get me some bacon and eggs, maybe?"

"She wants them fried firm," Zaharias said, coming into the kitchen, "in a sandwich. We'll need some fresh bread." He got the bacon out of the icebox and put it in a frying pan, carefully watching and turning it.

"She must feel better if she's hungry," he said happily.

The intercom buzzed again.

"Honey," the lady of the house said cheerily, "send Joan in here. I'd like to meet her."

Two double beds dominated the room and Babe Didrikson Zaharias was in the far one.

Twenty-two years had passed since her portrait had been painted, but her pillowed head looked much the same. Her brown hair was longer, softer. Time and laughter had etched lines around her eyes, but the same spark, the intensity and alertness burned in them still. . . .

"George and I started the Ladies' PGA in 1949," she explained. "I had this good golf game, but nothing to play in. There were three or four tournaments a year, but they'd come months apart. I was working most of the time, playing exhibitions, but we wanted this tour. We had to have players. We felt if we could get out and help some young players, we'd get them to play good so we could have competition.

"George would give them lessons. Then they got good." She sat up on the pillow. "'Forget the lessons, George,' I told him, 'they're getting tough.'"

"It's given Babe a big thrill to watch this thing grow," Zaharias said. "While she was playing in it, the most she could win was $1,000, and she could have made four times that much in exhibitions in four days. But money has never moved Babe much. She likes to play in tournaments. She likes the crowds, the competition."

"It's just like being on the stage," Babe said excitedly. "I get such a kick out of playing for people." She smiled girlishly as if the applause of the gallery were ringing in her ears. . . .

A TWO-TIME Olympic gold medalist in track and field, Zaharias dominated women's golf in the early Fifties and helped found the LPGA.

1973 | TOM WEISKOPF rode shotgun with mad hatter Johnny Miller at the
British Open before Weiskopf copped the claret jug. | *Photograph by* GRAHAM FINLAYSON

1900s | HORACE RAWLINS, who won the first U.S. Open in 1895, sat below bow-tied
four-time champ Willie Anderson and '06 winner Alex Smith (right). | *Photograph by* USGA MUSEUM

1938 | AN EXPERIMENTAL camera caught Bobby Jones in the ball-squashing, tie-flying 1/100,000th of a second after impact. | *Photograph by* BROWN BROTHERS

1930 | NEW YORKERS gave Jones a ticker-tape parade after his British Open victory put him halfway to the Grand Slam. | *Photograph by* BROWN BROTHERS

THE TRUMP TOUR

BY MICHAEL BAMBERGER

With his Scottish roots and American billions, Donald Trump figured he had every right to build golf courses his way. Was he out to honor the game's traditions, or to bulldoze them?
—*from* SI, JUNE 12, 2007

M Y ASSIGNMENT, AS IT first came down to me from on high, was to play Trump's courses and write up the tour, and my goal at first was to avoid the owner. Donald Trump, everybody knows, is a career .400 salesman, and I was afraid he'd overwhelm me. I had met him once, in 2002, when I was covering the season-ending event on the LPGA tour, played at the Trump course in West Palm Beach, Trump International Golf Club.

The course looked beautiful, and by 2005 it was on the *Golf Digest* list of America's 100 Greatest Golf Courses, in 84th place. But it was the kind of course for which, to borrow a phrase, I have unaffected scorn: crazy expensive to build and maintain, with a man-made waterfall, a man-made mountain and miles of cart paths. And apparently Trump was feuding with his contractors and not paying them, which may have accounted for the colossal clubhouse still showing exposed wires and (in places) concrete floors. Trump gave me a tour of his unfinished Taj Mahal with a lieutenant at his side.

We arrived in the grand ballroom where there were massive windows overlooking the course. Trump said to me, "My decorator says I need drapes on those windows, but I kind of like the unobstructed views of the course. What do you think?"

I figured the drape budget was gone. Trying to be polite, I said, "With those views of the course, who needs drapes?"

Trump turned to his lieutenant and said, "The guy from SI has spoken—no drapes!"

It was as if Ely Callaway, another scratch marketing man who ultimately figured out a way to leave his mark on golf, was back from the dead.

When I showed up at the Trump National Golf Club, in New York's Westchester County, Trump was waiting in the XXL clubhouse. He was wearing a red baseball cap with the gold logo of his club on the front and one of those Little League adjustable straps, with the holes and the little plastic pegs, in the back. It was a rainy, gray day, but Trump was ready to go. We were a fivesome: Trump and me; Trump's friend Louis Rinaldi, who is in the pavement business; a young pro with LPGA aspirations named Bri Vega; and my friend Mike Donald, a former Tour player.

Rinaldi, a lefthander with a lot of swagger and a handsy scratch golf game, built all the cart paths on the course. Trump made him a member of the club and gave him a locker in the same row as those of Trump, Bill Clinton, Rudy Giuliani and Joe Torre. "Are these not the most beautiful cart paths you have ever seen in your life?" Trump asked Mike and me. "Look at this curbing. You won't see curbing like this anywhere else. I can play with anybody, chairmen of the biggest banks, any celebrity I want to play with. But you know something? I'd rather play with Lou. You can take Lou anywhere." Trump slapped me on the shoulder and said, "You understand." He went off and played his shot.

It was clear that Trump *loved* his Westchester course, in the vicinity of Westchester Country Club, site of an annual Tour event, and Winged Foot, where Trump is a member. He talked about an underground pumping system, the millions he spent on a waterfall, how much Clinton enjoyed playing there, how the Tour would like to move the Barclays Classic from Westchester Country Club to his course. He described in detail how he defeated Rinaldi one year in the final to win the club championship, which is amazing because Trump looked like a golfer who could maybe break 80 and Rinaldi looked as if he could break par anywhere, but strange things happen in golf, especially on your home course, and most especially when you've built it yourself. The design is credited to Jim Fazio, but Trump, by his accounting, had done a lot to shape every hole. It was obvious Trump believed the course also belonged on the *Golf Digest* list. "I have people coming up to me all the time saying my New Jersey course is the best course they've ever played, but I think this one is every bit as good and maybe better," Trump said.

At the turn he slipped into the clubhouse for a few minutes where a foot-high stack of tax documents awaited him. He signed a few of them with his distinctive, thick up-and-down signature and said, "Golf is a small part of my business. One, two percent. But you know why I spend so much time on it? Because I do what I want, and I like it.". . .

THE DONALD, who owned seven courses worldwide and wanted to build "the best ever" in Scotland, tended to business at Trump National in Bedminster, N.J.

1971 | THE FAN in the white fedora didn't seem to fancy Lee's chances as leader Trevino slashed his way to his first British Open win. | *Photograph by* BOB THOMAS

1969 | TOUGH-GUY TREVINO had a fighter's heart, a safecracker's touch and a disguise: His Merry Mex act led some to take him lightly. | *Photograph by* WALTER IOOSS JR.

2007 | CALIFORNIAN PAULA CREAMER went spikes-over-teakettle when the Old Course hosted its first women's British Open. | *Photograph by* WARREN LITTLE

1900 | A DISTAFF MEMBER dressed for duress at Shinnecock Hills, the first American golf club to admit women. | *Photograph by* USGA MUSEUM

GOOD LORD OF GOLF

BY SARAH BALLARD

In those days he was Lord Byron, the courtly Texan who in 1945 gave the game its version of Joe DiMaggio's hitting streak— a standard that would never be matched. —from SI, MAY 7, 1979

EVERY GREAT ATHLETE HAS, at the prime of his sporting life, a season or a year that stands out from the rest. It usually arrives in the midst of a series of good years, and a certain amount of time has to pass before its true size can be recognized. Babe Ruth's year was 1927. Bobby Jones's was '30. Don Budge's was '38. Ben Hogan's was '53.

Byron Nelson's year was 1945. He came as close that year as a golfer can to being unbeatable. He set records in '45 that are still on the books 34 years later and will undoubtedly be there 34 years from now. He played golf that other golfers found almost unbelievable. In that year Fred Corcoran of the PGA was able to line up 35 tournaments worth about half a million dollars. Nelson won 18, just over half of them.

Eighteen tournaments was 11 more than anyone had won in a calendar year. Eighteen tournaments in a year is five more than any golfer has won since. Furthermore, Nelson finished second seven times in 1945. His prize money, most of it in war bonds, was $52,000, half again as much as his own record the previous year. (That $52,000 was 10% of the total purse for '45. Ten percent of the total purse on the 1979 PGA Tour would be $1.3 million.)

It has often been argued that Nelson's record year could have occurred only at a time when the best of the competition was still away at war, but that overlooks Nelson's scoring, which was barely credible. In 120 rounds of tournament golf, Nelson's *average* score for 18 holes was 68.33. It is a record that has never been touched. Snead, with 69.23 in 1950, came closest. Hogan's 69.30 in '48 is next. Jack Nicklaus's best stroke average was 69.81 in '73, and that was for only 72 rounds.

During that year, Nelson was also working on another remarkable string. Between 1940 and '46, he finished in the money in 113 straight tournaments. Jack Nicklaus came closest to that record with 105 between '70 and '76. Also, it should be noted, in Nelson's day most tournaments paid only the top 15 places; during Nicklaus's string, 70 places were paid.

But the record for which Nelson will be remembered is the Streak. Between mid-March and early August, he won 11 tournaments in a row, a feat that is almost beyond comparison. The closest any golfer has come to the record in 34 years was when Nancy Lopez won five in a row in 1978.

Extraordinary feats in golf, rounds such as Johnny Miller's 63 in the 1973 U.S. Open at Oakmont, and Al Geiberger's 59 in the second round of the Memphis Classic in '77, are so unusual and so far beyond reasonable explanation that they are frequently said to have happened while the golfers were in a "trance" or a "fog," the implication being that the score was more the product of magic than an act of will. Nelson's '45 "trance" lasted five months and survived some heavy handicaps. Travel, for instance. Travel during World War II, no matter what the vehicle, was like a rush hour that lasted four years. Further, most of Nelson's travel was by train, which, even when things went according to schedule, required days instead of hours to get from one place to another. Nelson also won tournaments while playing benefits at a rate of at least one, more often two, a week wherever he went. He almost never was able to play a practice round.

The Streak began with a victory in the Miami Four-Ball tournament the second week of March. The next week, when he beat Snead in a playoff at Charlotte, Nelson sensed something unusual was going on. "I became confident," he remembers. "I realized I could do with the golf ball pretty much what I wanted to do."

After six wins, Byron told his wife, Louise, he wished he could blow up and get it over with. Instead he went to the golf course that day and shot a 66. People could scarcely believe what they were seeing. Tommy Armour, the famous Scottish pro who in the late '20s and early '30s won the U.S. Open, the British Open and the PGA, said, "Nelson plays golf shots like a virtuoso. There is no type of problem he can't handle. High shots, low shots, with the wind or across it, hooks or fades—he has absolute control of them all. He is the finest golfer I have ever seen."

Meanwhile, Nelson was aiming for the PGA Championship in July at the Moraine Country Club in Dayton. His loss the year before to Bob Hamilton had been an enormous disappointment and he was determined to redeem himself. But when he found himself two holes down to Mike Turnesa with only four holes to play in the second round, his hopes for redemption seemed about to go down the drain together with the longest winning streak—eight straight tournaments at that point—in the history of the game. . . .

WARMING UP before his victory at the 1939 U.S. Open, a 27-year-old Nelson put on a show for the boys at Philadelphia Country Club.

1996 – *today*

Tiger's Time

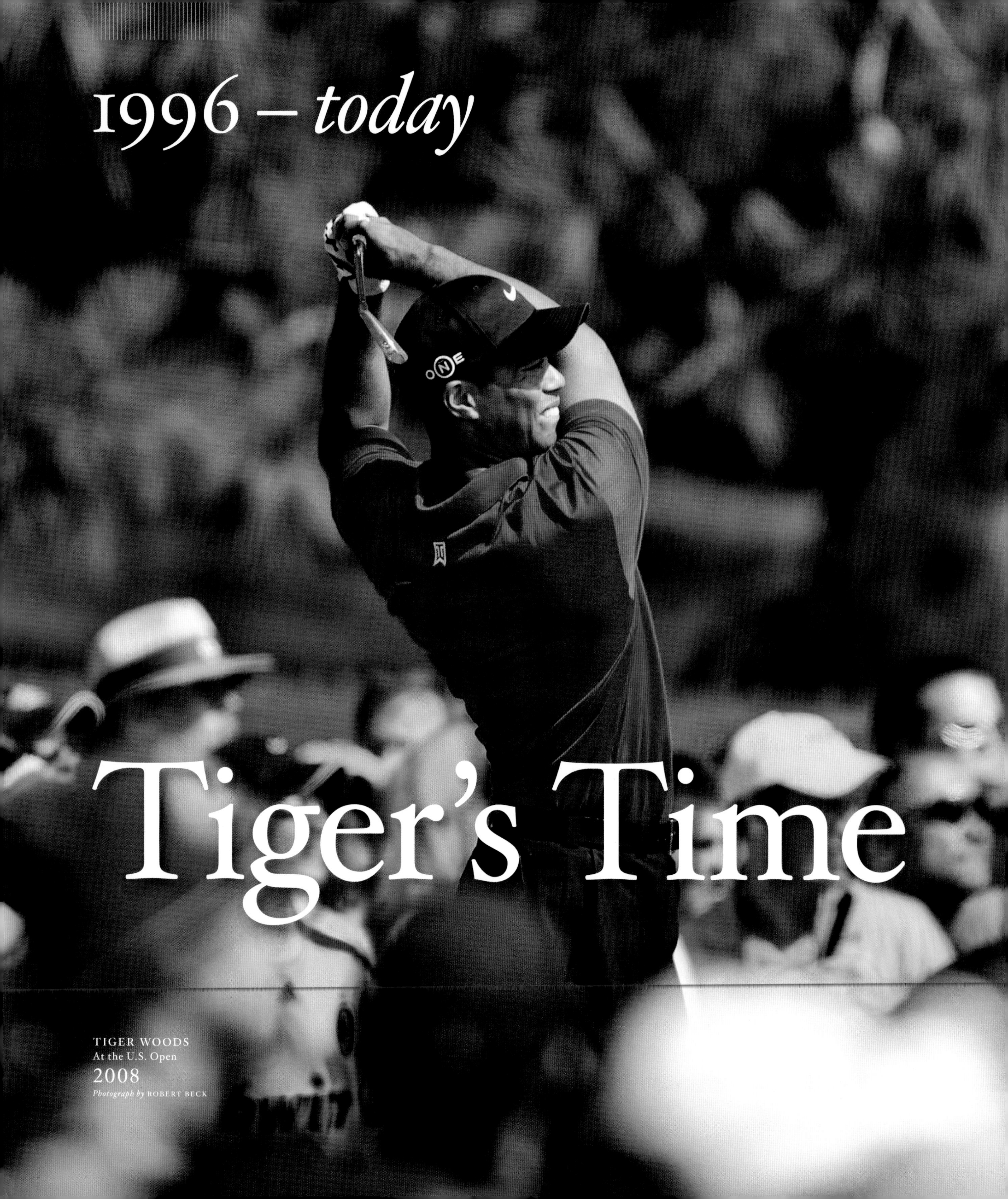

TIGER WOODS
At the U.S. Open
2008
Photograph by ROBERT BECK

THE ERA'S BEST

Tiger Woods

An international icon who could end up as the most accomplished performer in sports history, he was closing in on Jack Nicklaus's record of 18 professional majors as 2010 approached.

Annika Sorenstam

Ms. 59 not only shot the lowest round in LPGA history, she bagged 10 majors and 89 career victories (72 in the U.S.) and nearly made the cut in the PGA Tour's 2003 Colonial.

Phil Mickelson

In 2004 the short-game virtuoso shed the dubious title of Best Player Never to Have Won a Major by nabbing a Masters green jacket. He soon won a PGA Championship and another Masters.

Vijay Singh

The Fiji-born workaholic has been a chiseled model of endurance, topping the money list three times, winning three majors, and claiming 22 of his 34 Tour titles after his 40th birthday.

Ernie Els

The Big Easy ranks as the European tour's second-leading money winner of all time, having earned more than 22 million euros while raking in $34 million on this side of the pond.

>MILESTONES<

1996
TIGER WOODS
Turns pro, wins twice

1997
BEN HOGAN
64-time winner dies at 84

1999
GENE SARAZEN
Sand-wedge pioneer dies at 97

1999
PAYNE STEWART
Killed in an October plane crash

2000
100TH U.S. OPEN
Woods wins centennial Open by 15

2001
TIGER WOODS
Completes "Tiger Slam" at Masters

2002
SAM SNEAD
82-time tour winner dies

2002
BETHPAGE BLACK
First municipal U.S. Open course

2004
ARNOLD PALMER
Competes in 50th career Masters

2004
MICHELLE WIE >
Plays in men's PGA Tour event

NOW OPEN FOR PLAY

Pacific Dunes
BANDON, OREGON
2001 / Designed by Tom Doak
< THE SECOND OF FOUR COURSES THAT LURED PILGRIMS
TO A NEW GOLF MECCA IN THE PACIFIC NORTHWEST

Whistling Straits
HAVEN, WISCONSIN
1998 / Pete Dye

Friar's Head
RIVERHEAD, NEW YORK
2002 / Bill Coore & Ben Crenshaw

Nanea
KAILUA-KONA, HAWAII
2003 / David McLay Kidd

>> GOLF IN THE REAL WORLD <<

Happy Feat February 16, 1996 Adam Sandler stars in *Happy Gilmore*, >
a zany comedy about a hockey player who hits 400-yard slap shots and
joins the PGA Tour to save his grandmother's house from foreclosure.
With cameos from the unlikely trio of Bob Barker, Ben Stiller and
Lee Trevino, the film makes $41 million at the box office, though
Roger Ebert says Happy "doesn't have a pleasing personality."

Hootie and Boom-Boom September 4, 1996 A video for the Hootie
and the Blowfish hit *Only Wanna Be with You*, featuring a slew of
athletes including golfer Fred Couples, snags an MTV Video Music
Award nomination, but loses to the Foo Fighters' *Big Me*.

Training a Tiger? April 19, 1997 Soon after Tiger Woods wins his
first Masters, a *Saturday Night Live* sketch portrays Earl Woods as a
pushy dad who forced golf on his kid in hopes of making big bucks.
Tim Meadows, playing Tiger, says, "My first conscious memory is
my father Krazy-Gluing this plastic golf club to my hands."

Tournament Teas 1997 After guzzling the drink since the 1970s, the
King trademarks the Arnold Palmer, which is half iced tea and half
lemonade. If the bartender adds vodka, it's called a John Daly.

Bada-Ping March 14, 1999 In the first season of HBO's *The Sopranos*,
a neighbor invites Tony to the local country club. It seems Tony's
moving up in the world—until he realizes he's only there to give
his snooty playing partners the thrill of meeting a Mafia boss.

You Da Viniculturist! October 22, 2004 At *Wine Spectator*'s New
York Wine Experience, the two-time British Open champ scores
96—a good number in the wine biz—to nab the No. 8 spot in the
annual Top 100 for his Greg Norman Estates Shiraz Reserve 1999.

As a funeral procession
passed the course, a golfer
held his cap over his heart.
"That's mighty respectful,"
his caddie said. "It's the least
I can do," said the golfer.
"We were married for 30 years."

BEST SHOT

APRIL 10, 2005

Tiger Woods
With his ball against the second cut at
Augusta's par-3 16th, Woods starts his
chip 20 feet left of the cup. The ball
catches a slope and trickles into the
hole, giving him the outright lead as he
marches toward his fourth Masters win.

WORST SHOT

JULY 18, 1999

Jean Van de Velde
Needing only a double-bogey at 18 to
win the British Open, Van de Velde
hits a 185-yard two-iron into the fescue
along Barry Burn. After his next shot
finds the water, he makes a triple-
bogey 7 and loses a playoff.

> THE SWING
TIGER WOODS'S *wide takeaway, fast hips and core-muscle power drive the move that spurred Tigermania.*

> GOLF EVOLVES

A BETTER BERMUDA The Department of Agriculture grants a patent for TifEagle, a dense strain of bermuda grass with smaller, tougher blades, in 1999. Superintendents can now cut greens short enough to Stimp at Tour speeds without killing the grass.

HIGH-TECH BALLS In 2002 Top-Flite debuts the Strata, golf's first solid, multilayer ball. Within five years Titleist's three-piece Pro V1 dominates the Tour and wound balls go the way of the gutty and the dodo.

MAXED-OUT DRIVERS In 2004 the USGA sets maximum driver volume at 460 cubic centimeters, more than twice the size of the original Big Bertha.

RANGEFINDERS A 2006 USGA ruling okays laser and GPS distance-finders but lets each course set its own policy. Still banned on the PGA Tour (though permitted during practice rounds), such gadgets may *not* be used to measure wind or elevation changes.

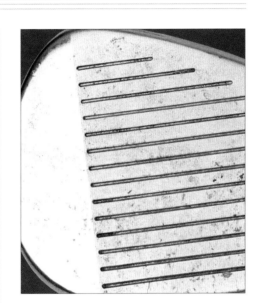

GAME CHANGER: V-GROOVES
To combat bomb-and-gouge golf, the USGA will make it harder to spin the ball from the rough. Irons made after Jan. 1, 2010, must feature V-shaped grooves rather than square or U-shaped grooves, which impart more spin.

>> FROM THE VAULT

"HOW HARD IS IT to root for Tiger, a golf god since he was two? It's like betting on the sunrise or rooting for Donald Trump to win the Publishers Clearinghouse sweepstakes. Rooting for Phil, on the other hand, is like watching a drunk chase a balloon near a cliff. You pray he gathers it in before you have to call the ambulance."

—RICK REILLY *in* SI, JULY 24, 2006

> ON THE NUMBER

$10.9 Millions in Tour earnings for Vijay Singh in 2004, still the highest single-season total in history.

14 Events played by Michelle Wie against men, including eight on the PGA Tour.

14 Wie's age when she played the 2004 Sony Open in Hawaii, making her the youngest golfer ever to play in a PGA Tour event.

20 Thousands of spectators who can jam the stands at the 162-yard, par-3 16th on the Stadium Course at TPC Scottsdale, home of the FBR Open, the Tour's best-attended, most raucous event.

29.5 Millions of golfers in America, according to the National Golf Foundation.

$40 Millions earned by Tiger Woods under his original Nike deal in 1996. In 2001 Woods re-upped for another five years and $100 million. In '06 he re-signed again for a reported $200 million over 10 years.

289 Strokes taken by 2007 Masters champ Zach Johnson, including a third-round 76, tying Jack Burke Jr. (1956) for the highest winning score at Augusta.

1995 | LOVE CONQUERED all but Ben Crenshaw at the Masters, as Davis Love III kept his eye on the ball but fell one swing short. | *Photograph by* JOHN IACONO

1964 | AFTER SEVERAL close calls, Ken Venturi won his first and only major at the 1964 U.S. Open, enduring 36 holes in 100° heat. | *Photograph by* JAMES DRAKE

2007 | PHIL MICKELSON missed a leaner for birdie on the 12th at Pebble Beach but went on to take the trophy at the AT&T, one of his 36 career victories—and counting. | *Photograph by* ROBERT BECK

CARE TO JOIN OUR LITTLE OLD GAME?

BY EDWIN SHRAKE

In which some sharks in Vegas waged the big-money battle of the year—with some highly unorthodox rules. —*from* SI, AUGUST 15, 1977

USING MONEY AS THE MEASURE of size, they played the world's biggest golf tournament in Las Vegas last week. You could take the purses from a dozen Greater Open Classics and still be barely within range of the amount of cash that 58 guys teed up for in the third Professional Gamblers Invitational at the Sahara Nevada Country Club.

The players bet each other more than $2 million during the three-day tournament. Nobody is quite sure who the winner was. A bookmaker from St. Louis came out well over $100,000 ahead, but he didn't win all his matches. The only one who did was Don Keller, who owns some drive-in cafés around Dallas. Keller is built like a monster squash and carries in his mouth a cigar that looks like an exhaust pipe. He couldn't break 90 if he had the only pencil on the course. But the way the PGI is handicapped, it is heart and luck that count, and Keller bounced his grounders onto enough greens to win the trophy—if there was one. "I think we ought to give Keller a pistol and a ski mask so he doesn't have to come all the way out here to rob people," said Jack Binion, who organized the tournament, made the matches and in his own wagers got "drown-ded," as the gamblers say.

Several of the country's king poker players were in the tournament. In fact Doyle Brunson, who won the World Series of Poker the last two years at Binion's Horseshoe Casino in downtown Las Vegas, not only inspired Jack Binion to start the PGI, but he also was one of its attractions to the other players.

Since early May, when he picked up $340,000 at the poker tournament, Brunson has lost enough money playing golf to pay the electric bill for a medium-sized nation. Nobody is supposed to have as much cash money as Doyle is said to have lost on the golf course in the last 2½ months. Brunson is a very high player who has the reputation of never flinching from a bet on the golf course or at the poker table. He has won millions at poker in games with the other king players and all challengers in Las Vegas, which is where you have to win at poker to be a king player.

But Brunson is what he calls "a bona fide golf degenerate." He is preparing a book, which he will publish himself, with the title *How to Win $1,000,000 Playing Poker*. "I may do a sequel called *How to Lose $1,000,000 Playing Golf*," Brunson said the night before the PGI began. He was eating watermelon in the Sombrero Room at Binion's Horseshoe. The next morning he was to play Butch Holmes, a commodities broker from Houston. The match had been rated even by Jack Binion, whose decision in such matters for the PGI is supreme. Doyle thought he ought to get a stroke.

The entry fee to play in the PGI was $1,900. That was broken into three $600 Nassaus on the three days of the tournament, plus $100 for carts and green fees. Binion got the idea for the PGI while playing golf in Fort Worth with Brunson, Pug Pearson, Sailor Roberts and other friends who have since persuaded Jack to retire from the game for a while. Binion's last game of golf cost him $11,000. But he thought high-playing golfers around the country should learn about each other. There are guys who shoot 105 but are willing to bet $6,000 per hole if the match is fair. The rules of the PGI allow players who shoot 100 or so to tee up the ball anywhere they please, including sand traps. The 90-shooters can roll the ball around to improve a lie. The 80-shooters are supposed to play it as it is. Stamping down the line of a putt is permitted. You can tote as many clubs as you wish. Doyle Brunson carries four putters. Also, you can use grease.

Johnny Moss, the famous poker player and golf gambler who is now in his early 70s and runs the poker room at the Dunes, recalls using grease from time to time in big games with Titanic Thompson. Brunson says he first learned about grease 12 years ago from a jeweler in Arlington, Texas. Pearson says he learned about it from Brunson. Mostly they use grease in Texas and in Las Vegas. Many a sucker has seen grease used in Florida or California or New York without realizing it.

Any sort of grease will do, although Vaseline is the most popular. What you do is smear grease on the club face before a shot. The grease cuts the spin off the ball. The ball is thus inclined neither to hook nor to slice, and it flies farther. At the PGI you might hear a player wondering whether to hit a dry three-iron or a wet five-iron. Of course the use of grease is against USGA rules. . . .

THE ENTRY FEES Amarillo Slim Preston and his fellow sharks shelled out were dwarfed by side bets, including one for "a Cadillac a hole."

2001 | FANS REACHED for the sky as Tiger Woods stole a stroke with a 60-foot putt on the 17th at TPC Sawgrass, a hole the pros love to hate. | *Photograph by* BOB MARTIN

1993 | PINING FOR his second U.S. Open title, Payne Stewart chipped away at Lee Janzen's lead but wound up two shots back. | *Photograph by* JOHN BIEVER

2009 | AFTER WINNING the last two majors of 2008, Dubliner Padraig Harrington escaped minor trouble at Doral. | *Photograph by* DARREN CARROLL

HOLD UP YOUR HEAD, TOM DOTY

BY BARRY McDERMOTT

He was a pretty decent player until the day when, for one brief shining moment, he was perfect. —*from* SI, JANUARY 17, 1972

GOLFERS ARE A CYNICAL group, a condition attributable to their frustrations. Perhaps no other game finds appeal from the notion that perfection never is to be attained or, once briefly experienced, never to be repeated. The vagaries of the swing confound the most accomplished, while the less gifted remain convinced that bone and muscle conspire to make them appear foolish. Gusts of wind baffle well-struck shots. Balls take peculiar bounces. And what golfer never has railed at the putt that wobbled?

Yet on a magic autumn afternoon in 1971 none of these tragic things happened to Tom Doty, at least not for a long while, and when his round was over he had not only the best golf story of the year but perhaps the best of all time. For during a four-hole stretch that unseasonably mild afternoon last November, he was the most talented golfer in the world. What Doty did that day defies credibility, and the feat well may have doomed his career. The mind cries out in protest, but he has witnesses and little apparent motive for deception.

On successive holes the 22-year-old assistant golf professional holed out a three-wood shot, a drive, a four-wood shot and a nine-iron shot. He went 2-1-1-2 with a double eagle, back-to-back holes in one and an eagle. And he may go through life burdened with his accomplishment, shadowed by whispers, for who among knowing golfers will believe him, and how can he hope ever to equal, much less surpass, the feat?

Manny Kantor, Peter Orofino, Harry Robbins and Frank LaPuzza always will believe him. They were playing that day with Doty at the Brookwood Country Club, located in the small Chicago suburb of Wood Dale, Ill., not far from O'Hare International Airport. These four businessmen, all in their middle 50s and 60s and longtime golfers, serve as testimony to the best golf ever recorded.

Doty finished with a round of 59, 13 under par on the 36-36—72, 6,435-yard course. But his final score means little.

Homero Blancas once shot a 55 while an amateur. The fact is, there is no known precedent for what Doty accomplished during that one remarkable four-hole stretch.

The round came on a Wednesday, shortly before Tom was to leave for a try at the winter tour in Florida, and it started innocuously enough with a bogey on the 3rd hole, where Doty joined the foursome of members. It hardly seemed possible that this would turn into the kind of game Doty fashioned in the pro-member tournament four months earlier. That time he set a course record with a 64.

Now at the 500-yard, par-5 4th hole Doty hit a solid drive down the left side of the fairway. "It was a fantastic drive," says LaPuzza, a 62-year-old bookstore owner. "My second shot was just a little bit ahead of his first." Doty pulled out a three-wood, aimed over a clump of 12 evergreen trees on the left and sailed a shot that seemed to explode off the club face. The ball hit just in front of the green, took a couple of hops and rolled into the cup for a double eagle.

The 5th hole at Brookwood is a weak par-4, 360 yards by the card, but it is a dogleg left, and plays less than that. A big hitter can carry a series of mounds and a bunker well out from the tee and put the ball on the green. With a strong wind at his back, Doty went for it.

"It's either on the green or close," Orofino said to Robbins as Doty's shot hooked toward the flag.

As they approached the hole and noticed that the ball was not visible, Kantor said, "I got a hunch. I wouldn't be a bit surprised if that ball went into the hole." And there it was, nestled at the bottom of the cup. Doty had played the previous hole with another ball, but after the double eagle he had put it back in his golf bag as a trophy. He did the same with this one.

As the group stood on the 6th tee, the golfers did not discuss the prospects of another hole in one. For one thing, the favoring wind of the 5th hole had shifted direction, and was now in their faces. And although the 6th is only 170 yards long, a par-3, the cup that day was near the back of the green. Doty took a four-wood from his bag to combat the wind.

"It hit a foot and a half in front of the hole," remembers Doty. His view of the tee shot was hampered by a bright sun, but he suspected what had happened, and it scared him. . . .

MIRACLE WORKER Doty, an Illinois assistant pro, used four balls to go 10 under par during his astounding four-hole streak.

pga
Level Footprints in Sand
MEN
Yds.
Par
MATCHES
WE
THEY
HOLE
Replace Divots Repair Ball Marks
WOMEN
Par
Yds.
Hc.
OUT
IN
HANDICAP
NET SCORE
COURSE RATING

2007 | TEEN STAR Rory McIlroy of Holywood, Northern Ireland, was a Hollywood story waiting to happen. | *Photograph by* ANDY LYONS

2005 | MICHELLE WIE generated massive buzz with her booming drives but struggled in her first year as a pro. | *Photograph by* DAVID BERGMAN

1989 | PUNCHING HIS ticket to history, Curtis Strange fired up the crowd and closed in on his second straight U.S. Open title. | *Photograph by* JOHN IACONO

1994 | DOWN THREE with three to play, Nick Price finished birdie, eagle, par, leap for joy to land the British Open crown at Turnberry. | *Photograph by* BOB MARTIN

BATTLE OF THE AGES

BY DAN JENKINS

The game's biggest names were dueling for the lead at the 1973 U.S. Open. Then a skinny blond also-ran started shooting the lights out. —from SI, JUNE 25, 1973

THERE IS NO BETTER WAY TO become an overnight, instant, presto, matinee idol in golf than to put yourself somewhere back in the Allegheny hills—about 12 coal mines and six roadhouses behind everybody seriously trying to win the U.S. Open championship, including a modest cast of Lee Trevino, Arnold Palmer, Jack Nicklaus, Gary Player, Julius Boros and Tom Weiskopf—and then come cruising along with your golden hair fluttering in the breeze, young, handsome and trim, and knock them all sideways with the most wonderful round of golf ever played. Meet Johnny Miller, the proud owner of a 63 at Oakmont, the young man who demolished the famous old course and all those famous people last Sunday with his miraculous finish.

What most guys do when they realize they are six strokes and 12 players behind starting the last round of the Open, especially when most of those players are immortals, is shoot a 73 or something, grab their $1,700 and head for the airport. But what Johnny Miller did was go out roughly an hour ahead of the leaders and birdie half the golf course—exactly half the golf course, nine holes—and turn in the lowest single round in the 73-year history of our most important tournament.

It was one of those days that will be remembered in golf until some vague time in the future when even-birdie barely makes the cut and the Open is played on Venus. For the sake of posterity let us examine Miller's round blow by blow, for there is not likely to be another like it for a few decades. It was simply exquisite golf; nothing less. No shots bouncing off hot-dog sheds or tree trunks or sailing out of bunkers into the cups. Just golf, the way it ought to be played by one of the true stylists on the Tour, a dashing young man of 26 with a fine big swing and easy tempo.

Here is how it went: a three-iron and a five-foot birdie putt on the 1st, a nine-iron and one-foot birdie at the 2nd, a five-iron and a 25-foot birdie at the 3rd, a sand shot and a six-inch birdie tap at the 4th, a six-iron and two putts for a par at the 5th, a three-iron and two putts for a par at the 6th, a nine-iron and two putts for a par at the 7th, a four-wood at the 8th that missed the green, followed by three putts for a bogey—his only lapse—and a two-iron and two putts for a birdie at the 9th. Miller had made the turn in 32, four under par.

"After I birdied the 3rd hole, I said to myself, 'Son of a gun. I'm even par,' and I thought, 'Well, maybe I've got a chance to get back in the tournament!' But when I birdied the 4th I got a little tight. I almost gagged on a couple of putts at the 7th and 8th but the easy birdie at 9 calmed me down."

Miller was so calm he began to strike the ball even better. Like this: a five-iron and two putts for a par at the 10th, a wedge and a 14-foot birdie at the 11th, a four-iron and a 15-foot birdie at the 12th, a four-iron and a five-foot birdie at the 13th, a wedge and two putts for a par at the 14th, a four-iron and a 10-foot putt for a birdie at the 15th, a two-iron and two putts for a par at the 16th, a wedge and two putts for a par at the 17th and, finally, a five-iron and two putts for a par at the 18th. That made 31 coming in, 63 in all.

Miller appeared unusually solemn as he blazed over Oakmont, ripping it to shreds. And there was a reason. In 1971 he nearly did the same thing in the Masters. He almost shot another surreal round to come out of nowhere and win. But with a few holes left he started warming to the crowd. Waving and grinning.

"I finger-walked," he explained. "Nodding at everyone. And I lost. I guess I didn't actually let myself think about winning this time until the 18th tee when Miller Barber told me, 'Baby, you got it now.'"

The victory was worth considerably more to Johnny Miller than the $35,000 first prize. His agent and manager, Ed Barner, quickly sat down in the clubhouse and totaled up the bonus money that would flow from his contracts with Ford, MacGregor, Sears, Air West etc., and came up with $49,000. "This year alone," said Barner proudly.

For a long while on Sunday it looked as if it would not matter what Miller shot because the whole world was busily winning the Open. There were three-way and four-way and five-way ties for the lead over the frenzied first nine holes involving the local pet, Arnold Palmer, and all kinds of other contenders.

Certainly most of the thousands were cheering for Palmer to win, which would have been a romantic thing indeed. There was a moment early in the round when Palmer led by himself, and later, when Miller had gone flying by, he found himself standing over a four-foot birdie putt. . . .

MILLER TIMED his miracle perfectly—a blazing 63 on Open Sunday before the leaders came down the stretch at rugged Oakmont.

2007 | MEXICO'S LORENA OCHOA, the pride of Guadalajara, shot past Annika Sorenstam to LPGA supremacy before she turned 25. | *Photograph by* ROBERT GALLAGHER

1956 | MICKEY WRIGHT was 21 when she got her first pro victory; six years later she pulled off a "Mickey Slam" by winning four majors in a row. | *Photograph by* HY PESKIN

2007 | A DECADE after his arrival as El Niño, The Kid, Sergio García was the Heartbreak Adult at

Carnoustie, where he missed a 10-footer for the claret jug. | *Photograph by* BOB MARTIN

MORE FUN THAN A BARREL OF MONTYS

BY STEVE RUSHIN

The author's jaunt to the auld sod proved that an ancient Scottish sport could benefit from being translated into Rushin.

—*from* SI, JULY 26, 2004

THE TRAIN TO TROON, LIKE the Firth of Forth, is more fun to say than to see. But that's a principal attraction of Scotland: With its firths and Forths and heaths and Perths, it makes everyone sound like Daffy Duck. Indeed, even before he hits the Glenlivet, the average American golf tourist finds himself fuzzy-tongued, boasting in some pub to Keith from Leith, "I'm thtarting to thwing like Tham Thnead."

Thtill—*still*—Scotland is more than the sum of its twin inventions: golf and Scotch. You just wouldn't know it while spending a week at the British Open at Royal Troon, where a couple was discovered late Friday afternoon in flagrante delicto in the fescue. To the golf-and-Scotch-addled witness, the scene demonstrated once again the enormous difficulty of getting up-and-down in the rough at Troon and, at the same time, called to mind one of David Letterman's Top 10 Punch Lines to Scottish Dirty Jokes. ("Number 1: She's in the distillery, making Johnnie Walker red.")

But the rest of the week was less T&A than R&A. Which isn't to say that *everything* comes back to golf and Scotch at the Open. It is, just as often, about golf and *beer*. The on-course tented pub at Troon was called, brilliantly, the Open Arms. And all week long at the Open Arms there flowed a constant tide of lager—a firth of froth. So, after firing a 68 on Friday, Briton Barry Lane came off the course with a new fan club. "A couple of guys had had a few beers and were singing 'Barry Lane' on the way 'round," recalled Lane, his ears still ringing with the refrain: *Barry Lane is in my ears and in my eyes / There, beneath the blue suburban skies.* . . .

Except that the skies were anything but blue that day. "It was raining *sideways*," noted Phil Mickelson, and when a BBC radio reporter boasted that his own socks were "weather-repellent," the phrase served, when repunctuated, as an eternal forecast for the Open: "Weather: repellent."

And it isn't just the weather that's uniquely British. Some Troon members coughed out their dental plates at the sight of Ian Poulter in Union Jack slacks and claimed that a man so brazenly attired would *never* be admitted to the grounds on any other week of the year. To which Poulter replied, plaintively, "How can you fault a man for his pair of trousers?" He was pleading, in other words, for fashion tolerance. He sounded like Mahatma de la Renta.

Then again, the Scots are not exactly in the fashion avant-garde. Glasgow's official tourism slogan, posted on placards at Troon, is GLASGOW: SCOTLAND WITH STYLE, which, if you think about it, says more about Scotland than it does about Glasgow.

And yet on Sunday, by way of penance, Poulter was fartin' through tartan, relieved to have shot 72 in his Scotch-plaid plus-fours. "The last thing you wanna do," he said, "is post an 80 wearin' tartan *troozahs.*"

Yanks and Brits are, as George Bernard Shaw observed, divided by a common language. It's not true that all visitors to Scotland inevitably sound like Daffy Duck. In fact, while watching Bob Tway, near the River Tay, in the land of tweed, you sometimes speak like Tweety Bird. This makes it a challenge to say "the train at Troon," which famously screams past the 11th tee box, while 747s take off from adjacent Prestwick International Airport, while the surf from the Firth of Clyde relentlessly pounds the beach that borders the course. In the middle of this cacophony, a lone ranger holds a stick that futilely whispers QUIET PLEASE. Inexpressibly poignant in his optimism, the ranger evokes that student standing before the tank at Tiananmen Square.

All of which makes the Open more fun than a barrel of Montys. Troon member Colin Montgomerie, as gray and brooding as the Scottish sky, was asked if playing in the British Open is as much fun as it looks.

"No," he replied. "Not at all. And anyone who says this *is* fun is joking. . . . This is a job. And a horrible one." As ever with Monty, you got the impression that he was partly putting you on—like that tent in the food court at Royal Troon that identified its fare as THE BEST OF BRITISH FOOD.

Certainly *watching* the Open is as much fun as you can have with your troozahs on. . . .

CHEEKY STREAKER Mark Roberts disrupted the 1995 British Open at St. Andrews; nine years later at Royal Troon, Ian Poulter Union-jacked up his slacks.

1966 | DOUG SANDERS found a crimson sweater to match his ruby spikes but lost a stroke when he misread a putt. | *Photograph by* WALTER IOOSS JR.

1986 | KNOWN FOR his knickers as much as for his gorgeous swing, Payne Stewart buckled when he missed at the Masters. | *Photograph by* JOHN IACONO

2006 | A RED FLAG beckoned golfers to safety beyond hungry bunkers at County Louth Golf Club in Ireland. | *Photograph by* ANTHONY EDGEWORTH

HURTS SO GOOD

BY ALAN SHIPNUCK

Playing on a broken leg, risking the rest of his year each time he hit a drive, the world's top athlete added a new chapter to the game's grand, still-unfolding history. —*from SI, JUNE 23, 2008*

TIGER WOODS HAS DEFINED his career in terms of major championship victories, and in turn they have defined him. Some wins have been monuments to his power, as when he obliterated the old Augusta National in 1997, and others have been tributes to his precision, such as the 2000 British Open, when he navigated the heaving earth of the Old Course without hitting into a single bunker. Woods has separated himself with clutch putting, as at the '06 PGA Championship when he canned a pair of 40-footers early in the final round, and he has dazzled as a tactician, taking apart Southern Hills one little swing at a time at the '07 PGA. Woods's unique skill set was on display again at last week's U.S. Open, but this victory was more visceral. It was all heart.

Playing for the first time since arthroscopic knee surgery two months ago, Woods was sore, stiff and rusty when he arrived at Torrey Pines Golf Course in La Jolla, Calif., a 7,643-yard brute that was easily the longest track in major championship history. Over four riveting rounds and a taxing 19-hole Monday playoff, Woods didn't play the golf course so much as brawl with it, his left leg occasionally buckling mid-swing, his face often twisted into a mask of pain, audible grunts and groans escaping after many shots. Yet this son of a Green Beret simply soldiered on. Woods snatched this Open with typically heroic flourishes, but his 14th major championship triumph was mostly about a palpable refusal to give in—to the pain, to an exacting course and to anyone trying to take a trophy that Woods considered to be rightfully his.

After four days of scrappy golf Woods came to the par-5 72nd hole on Sunday trailing Rocco Mediate by a stroke. A bad drive into a fairway bunker and a sloppy layup left him in the tangly right rough, 101 yards from a dangerous pin cut hard against a green-front pond. Woods muscled a wedge shot to within 12 feet, and our national championship was suddenly distilled into a moment thrilling in its simplicity: Make the putt or go home. One of Earl Woods's most famous quotes was actually a whisper into his son's ear at a critical juncture of a long-ago U.S. Amateur: "Let the legend grow." It grows, still. Woods buried the putt, setting up the 18-hole playoff with Mediate, a likable 45-year-old veteran with a bad back and loose lips and not the foggiest idea of what he had gotten himself into.

On Monday, Mediate battled bravely and actually outplayed Woods tee-to-green but he could not match his opponent's resourcefulness. Mediate was at even par and one stroke ahead playing the 18th hole but for the second straight day could only make a disappointing par. When Woods summoned a textbook two-putt birdie the two moved on to sudden death. On the first extra hole Woods played two flawless shots and Mediate finally cracked, going from a fairway bunker to greenside rough en route to a fatal bogey.

Mediate has long been one of Woods's most vocal fans. When they bumped into each other following the third round, during which Tiger had made two eagles and chipped in for birdie over the closing six holes, Mediate couldn't contain himself: "Are you completely out of your mind? Jeez-o, man!" On Sunday evening, following Woods's final-hole birdie, Mediate said, "I knew he'd make that putt. That's what he does." His opinion of Woods was only elevated during the playoff. "He is *so* hard to beat," Mediate said when it was over. "He's unreal."

For Woods the victory was deeply satisfying on any number of levels. This is his third U.S. Open championship but first in six years, and in the annals of the tournament he now trails only four-time winners Willie Anderson, Bobby Jones, Ben Hogan and Jack Nicklaus. With his 14 career majors Woods has crept ever closer to Nicklaus's epic total of 18, and it is mind-boggling to think that at 32 he is potentially one great calendar year away from attaining the unattainable. Then there is the Torrey story—Woods grew up about 90 miles from this celebrated municipal course and has been playing there since he was a kid and winning there since he was a teen. It is poetic that a player who was forged on the hardscrabble fairways of public courses has won his U.S. Opens at Pebble Beach, Bethpage and Torrey Pines, three layouts that are open to all.

Woods will always be most closely identified with the Masters because of the sociopolitical overtones of his breakthrough victory in 1997 and because the exquisitely manicured course allows him to display both his creativity and his power. The U.S. Open, however, is more reflective of what Woods is all about. It's a grinder's tournament, a nonstop stressfest. . . .

IN GRINDING PAIN that left him using clubs as crutches, Woods endured four rounds at Torrey Pines, plus an 18-hole playoff and sudden death.

FRED VUICH

1964 | DRIVEN TO his knees by a near miss at Augusta's 16th, Jack Nicklaus would drop the putt of a lifetime on the same hole 22 years later. | *Photograph by* MARVIN E. NEWMAN

2008 | SUFFERING FROM a bunker complex at the PGA Championship, Camilo Villegas rose to the challenge. | *Photograph by* CARLOS OSORIO

2008 | RICHARD JOHNSON escaped a world of trouble when the World Cup visited Mission Hills Golf Club in China. | *Photograph by* WANG JIAOWEN

HOLIN' ONE

BY JACK McCALLUM

For six men on a singular mission, chasing aces turned out to be golf in microcosm: the fruitless pursuit of perfection.

—*from* SI, JUNE 17, 1996

THERE ARE SIX OF US STANDING behind the tee box on the 17th hole of the Seaview Resort's Bay Course in Absecon, N.J. The flag is about 120 yards away, on the left side of the green, 20 feet behind a large sand trap. We are firing wedges, nine-irons, eight-irons and even a seven-wood or two into the early-morning mist, the idea being for one of us to hit the ball into the cup off the tee. Technically, of course, it would not count as a hole in one, because regulation aces have to be scored during regulation rounds. There is the story of one Lew Cullum of Largo, Fla., who in 1966 hit his tee shot into the lake on the 145-yard 11th hole at Yacht Club Estates Golf Club, near St. Petersburg, and followed it by depositing three more tee shots in the same place. His fifth shot, however, found the cup, thus earning him a 9 on the hole.

But I'm not expecting an ace anyway. Although two members of my group—Seaview head pro Matt Gillogly and assistant pro Andrew Rogers—each have had a hole in one (though not on the Bay 17th), I am positive it will not happen over the three-hour period set aside for our seemingly point-less endeavor. I have nothing to prove with this hole-in-one experiment except that I am not hole-in-one lucky. I've never gotten a hole in one, I never expect to, and I've never played a round in a group with anybody who did get one.

But I'm convinced there is a parallel universe out there, one in which holes in one are as common as mulligans: Hole in One World. Aces reported to *Golf Digest*, the hole-in-one clearinghouse since 1952 (the year the magazine began sending out report forms to every clubhouse in the country), range from about 38,000 to 42,000 per year. Newspapers regularly run reports of 80-year-old grandmothers and 10-year-old grandsons who "aced the 110-yard 12th with a three-wood." A number of insurance agencies make good money by providing hole-in-one insurance to tournaments in which cash prizes, automobiles, golf vacations or, in the case of the National Funeral Directors Association tournament, a casket is given away for aces. Indeed, there is nothing in sports that seems at once so remarkable and yet so pedestrian as the hole in one.

There's even one man who makes a living off his hole-in-one reputation: Mancil Davis, a fast-talking, wisecracking former club pro, who is now the director of event management for the National Hole In One Association. Davis, 42, played junior golf in Texas against Ben Crenshaw and Tom Kite and, in 1975, briefly tried the PGA Tour. He quit because, he says, "my caddie made more money than I did." Davis can't drive and can't putt, but what he can do is find the hole from the tee. The self-proclaimed King of Aces puts his hole-in-one total at 50, and that does not include, he says, the 10 or so he has made at corporate outings, in which he stays at one par-3 and fires tee shots at the flag all day, in much the same way my companions and I are doing right now. Davis's career path was set early. He had eight aces in '66, when he was only 12, and earned an appearance on *I've Got a Secret*, where he stumped the formidable mixed foursome of Bill Cullen, Henry Morgan, Bess Myerson and Betsy Palmer.

But no matter how I analyze it, 50 holes in one by one man (and that's not even the record)—not to mention 40,000 per year in a country that produces more duffers than dentists—seems like an unnatural conquest of the odds, which, by the way, are about 13,500 to 1 for an amateur golfer, about half that for a club pro and about 3,500 to 1 for a touring pro.

Davis says that psychologists have done tests on him and found that "my brain waves are different, much more positive, when I'm hitting a six-iron on a par-3 tee than when I'm hitting a six-iron from the fairway." Well, it figures that brain waves would be involved when you hit a ball that measures at least 1.68 inches in diameter into a hole that measures 4.25 inches in diameter from distances of 100 to 496 yards. (Oh, yes, there has been a 496-yard ace.) Or, as Mac O'Grady, the Tour's only certifiable spaceman, once said: "A hole in one is amazing when you think of the different universes this white mass of molecules has to pass through on its way to the hole."

I ask my hole-in-one partners if they think much about brain waves or different universes when they're on a par-3. "Right now I'm thinking about blisters," says my friend Bob Fink as he hits his 50th shot of the morning. It passes through several universes before landing in a sandy one in front of the green. . . .

DEFYING ONE–IN–13,500 odds, Richard Nixon did the deed with a five-iron on Bel-Air Country Club's 155-yard 3rd hole in 1963.

2004 | ONE OLD PRO said golf is simple—"You hit the ball, you go find it, then you hit it again"—but even that's sometimes easier said than done. | *Photograph by* CHARLES LINDSAY

1965 | WHAT APPEARED to be a casual Palmer-Nicklaus moment was actually a summit arranged by a master photographer, who felt "a little tension—the rivalry" between the men. | *Photograph by* WALTER IOOSS JR.

Acknowledgments

THESE PAGES are a tribute to the work of many brilliant writers and photographers, particularly those who have covered golf for SPORTS ILLUSTRATED starting with its debut issue in 1954. This book also attests to the talents of SI staffers and allies Linda Verigan, Don Delliquanti, Miriam Marseu, Steve Fine, Ed Truscio, Dick Friedman, Greg Kelly, David Dusek, Geoff Michaud, Dan Larkin, Bob Thompson, Karen Carpenter, George Amores, Natasha Simon, Leon Avelino and Julee Luu.

We owe thanks to the USGA's Rand Jerris, Robert Alvarez and Ellie Kaiser for their invaluable help with historical artifacts and photos. The same goes for Jack Peter and Mark Cubbedge at the World Golf Hall of Fame. Photographer David N. Berkwitz did a stellar job of shooting golf's treasures. Aaron Goodman's photo illustration of the alltime greats benefited immensely from the stylings of Allyson Vieira. The gorgeous driving range at PGA West played host to our Immortals' Invitational. The immortals looked sharp with help from Nike Golf; Cutter and Buck; Helen Uffner Vintage Clothing; Steve Auch at the Jack Nicklaus Museum; and golfknickers.com. Jane Fader, Mark Emerson, Mitchell Spearman, Christopher Wightman and Stephen Zadrozny made contributions to the project as well.

Rob Fleder, David Bauer and Walter Bingham provided perspective. Many thanks to Jim Herre for his expertise and good counsel. Special thanks to SI's managing editor, Terry McDonell, for his support and sharp eye.

Grateful acknowledgment is made to the following for permission to reprint copyrighted material:

Golf's Greatest Putt © 1954 by Grantland Rice
Used with permission of Henry Grantland Rice II
Conversation: Babe and George Zaharias ©1956 by Joan Flynn Dreyspool
Used with permission of Colleen Flynn Stein
Education of a Competitor ©1960
by Robert Tyre Jones Jr.
Courtesy of the family of Robert T. Jones Jr.

Images colorized by SI Imaging

Historic artifacts courtesy of the USGA Museum and the World Golf Hall of Fame, photographed by David N. Berkwitz

COVER CREDITS: FRONT *(Top to bottom, from left)*: Al Panzera, Stephen Munday/Getty Images, Robert Beck, Doug Pensinger/Getty Images; Augusta National/Getty Images, Michael O'Bryon, Jacqueline Duvoisin, Fred Vuich; Robert Beck, Tony Triolo, AP, Robert Beck; Robert Beck (2), Augusta National/Getty Images, Tim Graham/Fox Photos/Getty Images; Ezra Shaw/Getty Images, Marvin E. Newman, Jan Collsioo/AP, John Iacono; Darren Carroll, John Iacono, Robert Beck, Bettmann/Corbis; Robert Beck, David Bergman, Bettmann/Corbis, Robert Beck. BACK *(Top to bottom, from left)*: Bettmann/Corbis, AP, Bettmann/Corbis, Gary A. Vasquez/US Presswire; Fred Vuich, Stuart Franklin/Getty Images, Andy Lyons/Getty Images, Bettmann/Corbis; Michael O'Bryon, Gus Ruelas/Reuters, Bettmann/Corbis, Mike Ehrmann/Wireimage; Olivier Gauthier/DPPI/Icon SMI, David Cannon/Getty Images, Augusta National/Getty Images, Michael Cohen/Getty Images; Jacqueline Duvoisin, Stephen Munday/Getty Images; Bettmann/Corbis, Phil Inglis/Wireimage; Bob Thomas/Getty Images (2), Bettmann/Corbis, Ted West/Central Press/Hulton Archive/Getty Images; David Cannon/Getty Images, Michael Cohen/Getty Images, Scott A. Miller/Getty Images, Al Kooistra/Wireimage. FRONT FLAP *(Top to bottom, from left)*: Hulton-Deutsch Collection/Corbis, Ben Margot/AP, Andy Altenburger/Icon SMI, Pete Fontaine/Icon SMI; Jack Carroll/Icon SMI, David Liam Kyle, Doug Murray/Icon SMI, Kevin C. Cox/Getty Images. BACK FLAP *(Top to bottom, from left)*: James Drake, Augusta National/Getty Images, Darren Carroll, Hulton Archive/Getty Images; Jacqueline Duvoisin, Andrew Redington/Getty Images, Chris McGrath/Getty Images, Ross Kinnaird/Getty Images; Hulton-Deutsch Collection/Corbis, Bettmann/Corbis, Caryn Levy, Scott Halleran/Getty Images.

TABLE OF CONTENTS *(Top to bottom from left)*: James Drake, Michael O'Bryon, Malcolm L. Wister, John Iacono; Anthony Ravielli, Al Tielemans, Simon Bruty; Jacqueline Duvoisin, Walter Iooss Jr., Bernie Fuchs, Hy Peskin, Richard Jeffery, Neil Leifer, Fred Vuich.

ARTIFACTS: USGA Museum/David N. Berkwitz: 1, 37, 72-73, 96, 97, 122, 123, 172; World Golf Hall of Fame/David N. Berkwitz: 8-9, 36, 48-49, 96, 172, 173, 179, 202, 203, 235, 296.

PICTURES: Bobby Jones Collection/MARBL: 2-3; USGA Museum: 16-17, 42; Wireimage: 18; Getty Images: 19, 20-21, 30, 68-69, 114, 120, 176, 177, 180, 186, 190, 219, 225, 246, 249, 268; Corbis: 28-29, 62, 82, 106, 124, 130, 234; Globe Photos: 43; AP: 51, 94, 288; DPPI/Icon SMI: 52; MillerBrown: 103; Time & Life Pictures/Getty Images: 111, 156; Atlanta Journal-Constitution: 137; Keystone Features/Getty Images: 153; AFP/Getty Images: 211; Legendary Golf Links of Ireland: 237, 282-283; Color China Photos/Zuma Press: 289; Bullfinch Press: 292-293.

GATEFOLD: Photo illustration by Aaron Goodman Studios, Inc. AP (Hogan, Nelson); Robert Beck (Sorenstam); Bettmann/Corbis (Vardon, Jones); John Biever (Woods, background scoreboard); David Cannon/Getty Images (Ballesteros); Corbis (Sarazen, Hagen); Stephen Green-Armytage (Nicklaus); James Hardie/Hulton Archive/Getty Images (Young Tom Morris); John Iacono (Watson); Walter Iooss Jr. (Trevino); Keystone Pictures/Courtesy of Mrs. R.L. Brown (Zaharias); LPGA (Wright); Neil Leifer (Casper); Hy Peskin (Snead); USGA Museum (Old Tom Morris); John G. Zimmerman (Palmer). On flap: USGA Museum (Old Tom Morris), Bob Martin (Woods)

MOVIE POSTERS *(Clockwise from far left)*: Orion Pictures/Everett Collection, 20th Century Fox/Everett Collection, MGM/Everett Collection, Everett Collection, Universal Pictures/Everett Collection, Everett Collection, Warner Bros./Everett Collection, Everett Collection (3), DreamWorks Distribution/Everett Collection

IN THE BEGINNING *Milestones*: Hulton Archive/Getty Images; *Now Open*: Bettmann/Corbis; *Real World*: Bettmann/Corbis; *Best Shot*: USGA Museum; *Worst Shot*: Bob Thomas/Popperfoto/Getty Images; *The Swing*: USGA Museum (6); *Game Changer*: S. Saffery

THE GOLDEN AGE *Milestones*: Augusta National/Getty Images; *Now Open*: John G. Zimmerman; *Real World*: Bettmann/Corbis; *Best Shot*: USGA Museum; *Worst Shot*: Bettmann/Corbis; *The Swing*: Courtesy of the family of Robert T. Jones Jr. (8); *Game Changer*: Al Panzera/Fort Worth Telegram

HALL OF FAMER Louise Suggs drove into the sunset.

DAWN OF THE TOUR *Milestones*: Bettmann/Corbis; *Now Open*: Jamie Squire/Getty Images; *Real World*: CBS/Landov; *Best Shot*: AP; *Worst Shot*: Bettmann/Corbis; *The Swing*: Leonard Kamsler (8); *Game Changer*: Loomis Dean/Time & Life Pictures/Getty Images

THE RISE OF ARNIE AND JACK *Milestones*: AP; *Now Open*: James Schnepf; *Real World*: Carroll Seghers II/Globe Photos; *Best Shot*: Art Shay; *Worst Shot*: Art Rickerby; *The Swing*: Leonard Kamsler (8); *Game Changer*: Courtesy of PING

THE POLYESTER ERA *Milestones*: Bill Mahan/Leviton Atlanta; *Now Open*: Fred Vuich; *Real World*: NASA (Shepard), PictureNet/Corbis (TV); *Best Shot*: Gerry Cranham; *Worst Shot*: Gerry Cranham; *The Swing*: Leonard Kamsler (8); *Game Changer*: Scott Halleran/Getty Images

A GROWING GAME *Milestones*: Jacqueline Duvoisin; *Now Open*: David Cannon/Getty Images; *Real World*: Courtesy of Incredible Technologies; *Best Shot*: John Iacono; *Worst Shot*: Steve Powell; *The Swing*: Leonard Kamsler (8); *Game Changer*: Ben Van Hook

TIGER'S TIME *Milestones*: Robert Beck; *Now Open*: Henebry Photography/Courtesy of Bandon Dunes; *Real World*: Universal Pictures/Everett Collection; *Best Shot*: Al Tielemans; *Worst Shot*: Ben Curtis/AP; *The Swing*: Fred Vuich (8); *Game Changer*: Erick W. Rasco

TIME INC. HOME ENTERTAINMENT: Richard Fraiman, PUBLISHER; Steven ████████; ██████ ████████; ████ ██████, EXECUTIVE DIRECTOR, MARKETING SERVICES; Tom Mifsud, DIRECTOR, RETAIL & SPECIAL SALES; Peter Harper, DIRECTOR, NEW PRODUCT DEVELOPMENT; Laura Adam, ASSISTANT DIRECTOR, BOOKAZINE MARKETING; Joy Butts, ASSISTANT PUBLISHING DIRECTOR, BRAND MARKETING; Helen Wan, ASSOCIATE COUNSEL; Alexandra Bliss, BRAND & LICENSING MANAGER; Allison Parker, ASSOCIATE BRAND MANAGER; Anne-Michelle Gallero, DESIGN & PREPRESS MANAGER; Susan Chodakiewicz, BOOK PRODUCTION MANAGER